Should Prometheus Be Bound?

Also by Philippe de Woot

LA FONCTION D'ENTERPRISE

POUR UNE DOCTRINE DE L'ENTREPRISE

STRATÉGIE ET MANAGEMENT

HIGH TECHNOLOGY EUROPE

MANAGEMENT STRATÉGIQUE DES GROUPES INDUSTRIELS (*with X. Desclé*)

LA GLOBALISATION: Babel ou Pentecôte? (*with J. Delcourt*)

EDUCATION FOR EUROPEANS (*with P. Cochinaux*)

LE MÉTIER DE DIRIGEANT (*with O. Lecerf and J. Barraux*)

EUROMANAGEMENT: A New Style for the Global Market (*with R. Calori and H. Bloom*)

A EUROPEAN MANAGEMENT MODEL: Beyond Diversity (*edited with R. Calori*)

Should Prometheus Be Bound?

Corporate Global Responsibility

Philippe de Woot

First published 2005 by
PALGRAVE MACMILLAN
Houndmills, Basingstoke, Hampshire RG21 6XS and
175 Fifth Avenue, New York, N.Y. 10010
Companies and representatives throughout the world

PALGRAVE MACMILLAN is the global academic imprint of the Palgrave Macmillan division of St. Martin's Press, LLC and of Palgrave Macmillan Ltd. Macmillan® is a registered trademark in the United States, United Kingdom and other countries. Palgrave is a registered trademark in the European Union and other countries.

ISBN-13: 978–1–4039–4887–8
ISBN-10: 1–4039–4887–9

This book is printed on paper suitable for recycling and made from fully managed and sustained forest sources.

A catalogue record for this book is available from the British Library.

Library of Congress Cataloging-in-Publication Data
Woot, Philippe de.
   [Responsabilité sociale de l'entrepris. English]
   Should Prometheus be bound? : an essay on corporate social responsibility / by Philippe de Woot.
     p. cm.
   Includes bibliographical references and index.
   ISBN 1–4039–4887–9 (cloth)
   1. Social responsibility of business.   2. Corporate culture.
   3. Sustainable development.   I. Title.
   HD60.W66513 2005
   174'.4—dc22   2005040026

10   9   8   7   6   5   4   3   2   1
14   13   12   11   10   09   08   07   06   05

Printed and bound in Great Britain by
Antony Rowe Ltd, Chippenham and Eastbourne

Contents

Preface

Why Prometheus? Because he incarnates the creative entrepreneur who brings to mankind material progress, but also because he renders visible all the ambiguity of progress that lacks a clear purpose. He steals from the Gods to offer to mankind: 'Fire which liberates', 'The spring of creativity', 'Mastery of all the arts' and 'An infinite way forward'. But he is damned.[1]

Prometheus is audacity, vision, the extraordinary power of action and innovation found in successful companies. But he is also the cursed hero who questions us about the purpose of progress. He has 'delivered mankind' but is himself chained, and each morning an eagle arrives to peck at his liver. He is a Titan, but a condemned Titan. Why?

This question arising from the past reasserts itself with intensity today.

Never in the history of mankind have we created so much wealth, but poverty continues to grip so many throughout the world.

Never has our scientific understanding been so great but our planet so threatened.

We have invented effective political institutions such the nation state and democracy, but today the ways and means of economic development are beyond their control and on another plane altogether. The economic acceleration is such that we must question whether we still have any control over it.

In spite of its indisputable successes, our development model has become the target of increasing contestation, of a well-articulated ideological opposition and of social struggles that are clearly visible worldwide. We talk of the fundamentalism of the market, of the dominant ideology and of imperialist globalization.

What has happened?

* * *

The theme of this book is as follows. Companies are working according to a development model that is becoming unsustainable in many respects. To correct this they must undergo a profound change of culture and strategy. This can only happen if they are supported, on a global scale, by public policies that allow the emergence of a sustainable development model. This thesis is based on the following observations.

First, the firm is the chief agent of economic and technical progress. With its creativity and capacity to innovate, the firm shoulders the Promethean task of bringing material progress, the source of much other progress, to mankind.

For a long time it has been presumed that the actions of the firm automatically serve the common good, thanks to the virtues of the market and its famous 'invisible hand'. Today this link is becoming much less clear. Globalization, the growth of the technosciences and the lack of worldwide regulation confer on firms a power to act that is without precedent. They exercise this power according to their own criteria: profitability, competitiveness and the race for market share. In the absence of global rules, this logic has become dominant and imposed on us a development model whose only purpose is its own effectiveness and dynamism. Led solely by instrumental logic, the model is ambiguous and paradoxical. At the same time as creating more wealth than ever and ensuring unprecedented economic growth, it pollutes, excludes, and encourages domination, social injustice and destructuring; it promotes a desperate race that no longer has any clearly visible purpose or *raison d'être*.

In becoming global our development model has revealed its limits and contradictions. Its extraordinary capacity to create wealth, its international dynamism, creativity and spirit of enterprise are producing undesirable systemic effects that worry some and cause revulsion in others.

So must Prometheus be kept in chains and lose his creativity and drive, of which the world has such a need? Or should we transform the model to make it more appropriate for remedying the problems of the twenty-first century?

When one is the principal actor and has enormous economic power at one's disposal, one must have the courage to question the basic premises behind the current model. To delegate this task to the public powers alone is to give up the civic dimension of the firm, to fail to see the need to broaden responsibilities. In a world that is rapidly evolving 'the kings will continue to lose their heads as long as they wear their crowns over their eyes rather than on their foreheads' (Rivarol, 1964).

Henceforth the firm must question the meaning of its actions, its *raison d'être* or purpose. It should know whether it is possible to act in a responsible way in a system that lacks responsibility, whether it is still possible to be legitimate while adhering to a model that is increasingly ambiguous and contested, and whether it is possible to retain ethics worthy of the name while playing an economic game that has none.

Second, those business leaders and managers who drive this model with energy and competence have difficulty understanding their critics. They feel that they are contributing to the common good by ensuring the success of their business. They have difficulty accepting that they are at least partially responsible for the negative fallout of the system they drive, and they see no need to question a development model that to them is the most efficient available and to which they have dedicated their best efforts.

However, the more enlightened of them are beginning to reassess the situation. They accept that they must take on more social responsibilities and address deviations in the system. That is why movements have emerged in Europe and the US to address these matters. One European movement, Corporate Social Responsibility, together with a number of management schools, has even founded an academy whose sole purpose is to improve and expand teaching and research in this domain.[2]

Will this movement be able to correct the model and orientate it towards sustainable development? Everything will depend on the fundamental conceptions that inspire the movement and the depth of questioning they provoke.

When a firm declares itself to be responsible, what does that mean? To say responsibility is to say ethics. To say social responsibility is to say politics. This perspective bring us to the purpose of the firm, its values, culture, and the wider consequences of its strategies and behaviour. This touches on the citizenship dimension of the development model that the economic players drive, but which in turn imposes the rules of the game on them.

By launching themselves into the realm of social responsibility, are firms not opening a Pandora's box? Do they realise that they risk going further than they would like and having to question the very model and logic that underpins them?

The firm can play a decisive role in sustainable development, but that presupposes a much more profound transformation than most business leaders imagine. There can be no sustainable development unless the firm broadens its *raison d'être* and abandons the conventional wisdom, which has resulted in one-dimensional thinking and locked the firm into a logic of means rather than ends. The firm will only become responsible if it transforms its culture by adopting new ethical values and engaging in political debate with the new players in the globalizing world.

The required changes demand profound reflection and go well beyond a new coat for an old system. If the movement for social responsibility just sticks new labels onto old practices it will not be taken seriously; if it puts old wine into new bottles it will be reduced to a public relations operation. The movement will only be credible if it renews the concept of enterprise and reassesses its role in the construction of our shared future.

It is not our intention to blame firms for everything that is dysfunctional in the world, or to suggest that they alone can cure the world's ills. Rather it is a question of clarifying the central role they could play in improving the system. It is also a question of suggesting how important it is for enlightened leaders to head the move in this direction, to convince their peers that change is both necessary and possible, and to provoke from that a chain reaction. 'Do you know what an enzyme is, or a catalyst? It is something which makes no material contribution, but which sets a process in motion' (Musil, 1961).

Is it only the largest companies that are concerned with this? Not if we are talking of purpose, values and culture. It is the *raison d'être* of the firm that is at stake, and that concerns all firms in all sectors.

If the subject is power, influence and concrete participation in the efforts to transform the model, most small and medium-sized companies will only be able to do so through their professional associations.

From this perspective the movement for social responsibility will be essential to the reform of the development model. However it will not be enough. Taking into account the complexity and size of the problems that exist at the global level, new forms of international governance will be indispensable if the aim is to reorient firms' creativity and power of action towards the common good of the planet.

A new orientation is suggested by the concept of sustainable development, and it is within this framework that the responsible firm can locate its actions. But it will not be sufficient to recite this new concept like a mantra, it must be made to happen.

* * *

When considering firms' responsibilities from the view point of aims and purpose, this book offers reflection rather than tools. It brings some basic concepts into the discussion of the integration of the firm into the city. It seeks to return to the most fundamental questions that for centuries have addressed the construction of humanism and the integration of economic action and social evolution. This is the justification for the book's occasional recourse to ancient myths and the wisdom of the ancients.

This book is a work of opinion and not a report on research. It is aimed more at encouraging debate than at demonstration. It discusses the meaning of our development model rather than offering a theoretical analysis of its modes of operation. More systematic approaches to the movement for social responsibility already exist, notably the excellent book in French by Chaveau and Rosé (2003).

As the subject area is particularly vast and complex, the themes presented here are shown in high contrast – black and white rather than light and dark grey. Readers should add shade to my propositions whenever they feel that the truth only resides in the nuances.

I ask the managers of firms not to take the criticisms of the system too personally. If I compare them to Prometheus, it is not by chance. They have the same spirit of initiative and innovation, courage and energy, and often self-interest is replaced by devotion and a sense of service. I simply suggest that they ask themselves why the ancients wanted to chain this Titan and limit the possible excesses of the progress he sought, and to consider the extent to which they are ready to transform the system they drive with such conviction, but whose deviations risk calling into question the legitimacy of their actions.

Acknowledgements

I would like to thank the European Foundation for Management Development (EFMD) that has initiated and supported the English translation of this book; the Bernheim Foundation, which originated this work. My thanks also go to Bertrand Collomb (president of Lafarge), Etienne Davignon (president of Corporate Social Responsibility Europe), Georges Jacobs (former president of UNICE—Union of Industrial and Employers' Confederations of Europe) and Daniel Janssen (president of Solvay), who agreed to comment on the first draft. I am grateful to Henri-Claude de Bettignies (professor at INSEAD), who for years in his programme AVIRA (a special top executive program, organized by INSEAD) has been posing these questions to international business leaders; Emilio Fontela (professor at the University of Geneva), who inspired the reflections on financial deviations; Jean Ladrière (professor at the University of Louvain), who suggests keys to a new humanism; Alain Touraine, for the light he sheds on modernity; the companies Lafarge, Shell, Daimler-Chrysler and Novo Nordisk, which demonstrate that change is possible despite certain problems along the way; and the *Financial Times*, from which I have drawn many significant facts, statements by executives and opinions on the evolution of progress. Last but not least, I thank Malcolm Stewart for translating the manuscript with intelligence and finesse.

PHILIPPE DE WOOT

Part I

Corporate Creativity and an Unsustainable Development Model

Prometheus: 'I have cured mortals of the pangs of death.'
The Oceanides: 'And what remedy did you find for them?'
Prometheus: 'A blindfold over their eyes.'

(Aeschylus, *Prometheus Bound*)

1
The Creative Enterprise

I opened up for them the treasures of the earth: they had gold and silver, they had bronze, they had iron, they had industry and the arts.

(Aeschylus, *Prometheus Bound*)

The entrepreneur: a cursed hero

To question the *raison d'être*[1] of the enterprise, and the model it inspires, is to question material progress, its orientation and its ambiguities. This topic has preoccupied human beings since the beginnings of civilization. Using Greek myths as our departure point we shall put it in its true perspective, which lies in man's creativity and anxiety.

In the founding myths of our culture the gods and heroes who contributed to material progress occupy an important place. The Greeks saw them as heroes, but heroes who were cursed. Since the dawn of time material progress has been seen as both beneficial and dangerous, as essentially ambiguous.

The story of Prometheus is that of an entrepreneur. This Titan has all the characteristics of an entrepreneur: he sees the progress that fire will bring to mortals; he takes the risk of stealing it from the gods; he has the energy to do it and to convince humankind to make use of it. For this he is made a hero, but the gods punish him for it and chain him to a rock, and each morning an eagle comes to prey on his liver.

The same is true of Hephaistos (Vulcan), the god of fire and metalcraft who makes tools, arms and jewellery. He is lame and rarely leaves his cavern, which for a Greek who is in love with light is a form of curse. He is married to Aphrodite, which is not in itself a curse but she becomes so bored with her technician of a husband that she often returns to Mount Olympus to deceive him with other gods.

Odysseus (Ulysses) is a hero. His odyssey reflects the commercial drive of the Greeks in the Mediterranean. He is the marketing man of antiquity – astute, audacious, enterprising. This 'man with a thousand wiles' is a cursed hero whom the Gods forbid to return to his homeland and condemn to constant wandering.

Jason pursues wealth: the Golden Fleece. With his Argonauts he sets sail to steal the fleece. But his spirit of enterprise condemns him most cruelly. His wife kills their children and disappears with a god. One more cursed hero.

Hercules represents the myth of development. He is less brilliant than Prometheus but he will become a god, although this does not prevent him from coming to a bad end. He developed the world through his work, but the tunic of Nessus brings a tragic end to his existence. Death from overwork? Is he suffocated by an ambition to bring about development too quickly?

Finally, Icarus brings technical progress. He achieves the ancient dream of man to fly like a bird, but he loses his life.

The creators of material progress are Titans, heroes and gods. But why are they cursed?

Let us look a little closer at Prometheus and his creative impulse. In his tragedy *Prometheus Bound*, Aeschylus questions the purpose of development and material progress. He shows both the positive aspect of and his powerlessness to give a meaning to human destiny. Chained to his rock, Prometheus speaks of his work and for the first time sings of the spirit of enterprise and innovation:[2]

> ... but listen to the tale
> Of human sufferings, and how at first
> Senseless as beasts I gave men sense, possessed them
> Of mind ...
> In the beginning, seeing they saw amiss,
> And hearing heard not, but, like phantoms huddled
> In dreams, the perplexed story of their days

Confounded; knowing neither timber-work
Nor brick-built dwellings basking in the light,
But dug for themselves holes, wherein like ants,
That hardly may contend against a breath,
They dwelt in burrows of their unsunned caves.
Neither of winter's cold had they fixed sign,
Nor the spring when she comes decked with flowers,
Nor yet of summer's heat with melting fruits
...But utterly without knowledge
Moiled, until I the rising of the stars
Showed them and when they set, though much obscure.
Moreover, number, the most excellent
Of all inventions, I for them devised,
And gave them writing that retaineth all,
The serviceable mother of the Muse.
I was the first that yoked unmanaged beasts,
To serve as slaves with collar and with pack,
And take upon themselves, to man's relief,
The heaviest labor of his hands: and I
Tamed to the rein and drove in wheeléd carts
The horse, of sumptuous pride the ornament.
And those sea-wanderers with the wings of cloth,
The shipman's wagons, none but I contrived.
These manifold inventions for mankind
I perfected....
But hear the sequel and the more admire
What arts, what aids I cleverly evolved.
The chiefest that, if any man fell sick,
There was no help for him, comestible,
Lotion or potion; but for lack of drugs,
They dwindled quite away; ...
...and I purged
The glancing eye of fire, dim before,
And made its meaning plain. These are my works.
Then, things beneath the earth, aids hid from man,
Brass, iron, silver, gold, who dares to say
He was before me in discovering? ...
And in a single word to sum the whole—
All manner of arts men from Prometheus learned.

What a cry of admiration for the undertakings of which man is capable. Clearly what we have here is the Neolithic revolution: the major innovations, writing, the calendar, livestock farming, agriculture, the start of metalworking, townships – all are in this text. Reason and the power of thought: the application of intelligence to the external universe, time management and mathematics – 'the queen of all knowledge' – are evoked, as well as production and consumer goods and even conspicuous consumption – 'the pride of kings'.

Prometheus declares himself the agent of progress and development. He has opened for man an 'infinite pathway', he has given him 'a creative source' and initiated an irreversible movement. He broadcasts his justifiable pride in having brought to mankind so many 'marvels'. (It is interesting to note that Marx showed the same admiration for economic and technical progress: 'in the course of a barely secular class domination, the capitalist bourgeoisie created wonders quite different from the Egyptian pyramids, the Roman aqueducts or the Gothic cathedrals...' See Marx, 1848.)

At the start of his play Aeschylus presents this incredible set of innovations in terms of the progress of man. But then the second aspect of the drama emerges – an interrogation of the meaning and limits of material progress: 'My name is the seer, he who knows, Prometheus the subtle...he who saves mankind...I have cured mortals of the pangs of death.' And when the choir of the Oceanides, amazed at this extraordinary assertion, ask him 'but what remedy have you found for them?', Prometheus can only answer 'a blindfold, blind hope'.

From the dawn of economic life, therefore, it has been apparent that material progress is not the only remedy for the ills of mankind, that it is only one form of human progress and does not answer the essential questions. The gods have not accepted the risk of technical progress with no clear *raison d'être*. 'Fire, our dazzling privilege, in the hands of ephemeral beings.'

The unfortunate Prometheus is chained to a rock, and each morning the eagle, as it eats away at his liver, reminds him of 'the pangs of death'. But he still cannot resist dreaming. Have all his efforts failed to make mankind happy? 'Here comes the sound of wings, a flight of sparrows close to me and the sky beaten with feathers, sings gently.' Prometheus identifies himself with the dynamic of scientific and technical progress for humanity: fire, knowledge, the arts, medicine: In spite of his damnation he only gives a one-dimensional version. Already 'the unidimensional thinking' of conventional wisdom.

The chorus and the gods personify questioning about the ambiguities, meaning and purpose of technical progress. They see the dangers and possible excesses. But Prometheus cannot give up: 'Listen still to other marvels...' The chorus continues: 'You wished to help mortals, you forgot yourself, but your hour will come; one day you will have the power of Zeus.' What temptation!

Prometheus answers: 'Not yet, for beyond art, beyond cunning and intelligence, destiny commands.' All he has left is blind hope, hubris and a lack of moderation. When the chorus reproach him for his pride he retorts: 'Let the lightening burn me with its flame, let the thunder bellow in the bowels of the earth, let Zeus unchain his most powerful forces, shake the world and bring it into chaos, nothing will make me weaken.' Then Hermes the wise, the god of merchants and thieves, says to him: 'You have not learnt wisdom, Prometheus, your heart is growing hard; the pride of the mad is a poor power.'

In summary, the tragedy of Prometheus raises the question of whether ephemeral human beings can become masters of technical progress without securing its purpose and submitting it to the larger vision of the common good. This is the question that in various forms has been asked throughout history.

Innovation and creative destruction

If one were to observe successful firms over a period of five to ten years it could be seen that not a single one had failed to adapt, transform or renew itself. Each one would have evolved and innovated, be it in terms of its products, markets, procedures or organization, marking its actions as dynamic and creative.

Under the spur of competition and technical evolution, the successful firm is not content simply to produce and distribute its goods or services. It constantly renews them and seeks to evolve, to create the new. Initiative and creativity form the pivot of its undertaking. In the market economy the firm is the agent of economic and technical evolution. It is the firm that brings it about and fashions it into its most concrete form. Vision or simple descriptions are not enough – it must be done, it must be implemented.[3]

Schumpeter has shown very convincingly that economic development is dependent on innovation and that the agent for this is an
unusual personality: the entrepreneur. This person has very specific
qualities: a vision of progress, the energy and taste for risk required
to put ideas into practice, a power of conviction that is strong
enough to secure the necessary support and resources. Through its
creativity the innovative entrepreneurial firm transforms the nature
of competition. A simple price contest becomes a drive for innovation and technical progress. The competition that really counts is the

> competition of new goods, new methods, new supply sources,
> new forms of organization (e.g. control of larger units), in other
> words, competition that commands a decisive cost or quality
> advantage and which affects not existing firms' profit margins
> and volume of output, but their very foundations and existence.
> Just as bombardment is far more effective than battering down a
> gate, so this form of competition is much more effective than the
> other. So much greater is its significance that the speed at which
> competition... [proceeds is] relatively unimportant because the
> powerful mechanism for raising production and cutting prices
> long term is quite different.
>
> The problem generally taken into consideration is that of estab-
> lishing how capitalism manages the existing structures, whereas
> the important problem is to discover how it creates, and then
> destroys, its structures.
>
> As long as he [*sic*] remains unaware of this fact, the researcher is
> devoting himself to a meaningless task. But, as soon as he
> becomes conscious of it, his view of capitalist practices and their
> social consequences becomes considerably modified.
>
> At the same time... the traditional concept of the working of
> competition is thrown overboard. Economists are at last beginning
> to take off the blinkers which prevent them from seeing anything
> other than price competition. Once the competition of quality
> and sales effort are admitted into the sacred circle of theory, price
> variation ceases to occupy its dominant position. (Schumpeter,
> 1949)

This is the famous process of creative destruction.

At the end of his life Schumpeter seemed to believe that the specific role of the entrepreneur was becoming useless:

- Progress would become mechanized, innovation would become a routine, and the vision of the possibilities of progress would be replaced by calculation.
- There would be no more resistance to change and the energy needed to overcome it would not be required.
- Obstacles to innovation would arise without the entrepreneur having taken a grip on them: social forces, the official control of prices, the hostility of government bureaucracy ...

We all know that that was not the case in the second half of the twentieth century. On the contrary, the pace of innovation accelerated, the capacity for conducting projects developed greatly and routine did not replace creativity.

Scholars at the University of Louvain (Dupriez, 1949, 1959; de Woot, 1962; de Woot and Desclée, 1984), and more recently the American economist Baumol (2002), have shown that it is not only the individual entrepreneur who brings about innovation. The firm has taken on much of this role and ensures that this type of progress will continue to be collective and systematic. The successful firm is endowed with the qualities of the entrepreneur and with a capacity for innovation that is often deployed on a global scale. It knows that its success and survival depend on it. This confirms Schumpeter's assertion that 'enterprise means changing the existing order'.

The reality of economic and technical development is one of major innovations, often put in place by individual entrepreneurs but then rapidly taken over by the groups of entrepreneurs that comprize firms. Today the names of Ford, Singer, Campbell, Solvay, Lafarge, Michelin, Renault, Cockerill and Morgan no longer designate the creative entrepreneurs who founded them, but firms with collective capacities that reflect the qualities of their founders.

By becoming collective, the qualities of vision, risk and conviction in firms have considerably increased. *Vision* has become an essential element of the strategy of the firm and its dynamism. When potential progress is translated into a realistic vision that is shared by its employees, the firm, instead of being pushed by the past, is drawn into the future. And that makes all the difference in terms of creativity, motivation and dynamism. Think of the innovations in software born of the vision of Bill Gates of Microsoft. Think of the low-cost airlines and the visions of the creators of Southwest Airlines, Virgin and Ryanair. Consider too the visions based on decoding the human genome, the coming of age of digital technology, the opportunities opened up by space exploration and the spread of wireless communication.

The taste for *risk taking* and the energy needed for enterprise have also become a collective reality. Economic progress results from huge gambles, for example the investments recently agreed by the European telecommunications industry for third-generation mobile telephones include more than €100 billion just to obtain the necessary licences, to which must be added tens of billions more for the infrastructure. No one can say how long it will take to write off these enormous sums. The same gamble is taken in respect of space exploration, renewable energy, supersonic flight, new medicines and so on.

The necessity of a *power to convince* continues to grow. In the case of communication media, for example, it is necessary to convince tens of millions of consumers to subscribe to broadband networks, television on demand and internet services. And launching new enterprises to exploit knowledge of the human genome will require enormous sums of money.

Such innovative efforts are no longer down to individual entrepreneurs, but depend on organizations, systems and powerful groups. Later we shall see how firms equip and organize themselves in order to develop and maintain within them these qualities and to build a capacity for innovation, which remains the major competitive weapon and the principal source of economic development.

Without doubt we are now too used to it to remain astonished, but material progress in developed countries over the past two centuries is without precedent in human history. The progression from horse-drawn carriage to the railway and then the car and the aeroplane happened in less than a century. It is to the spirit of enterprise that we owe the extraordinary development of communication and information technology, energy sources, medical advances, sources of finance, methods of distribution, progress in agriculture and the production technology that has substantially increased the productivity of workers.

In summary, at the heart of enterprise, under the pressure of competition, is creativity, change and renewal. As a recent illustration, here are the words used by the chief executive of Sony to describe the firm's tactics to regenerate its slowing growth: 'constantly reorientate the group, transform it, redefine it, shape the new technological generation, create trends, create a new industry, develop new products, adapt, improve, build' (Nakamoto and Bort, 2003). Similarly the head of Dell Computers, who advocates applying to services the methods of production that have been successful in industry, claims that 'everything can always be improved'.[4]

The fact that innovation has become more systematic does not mean that it has become either routine or foreseeable. It continues to depend on gifted individuals or teams operating in conditions favourable to change, and it is one of the great challenges for large firms whose size is often the source of bureaucracy, immobility and resistance to change. The source of innovation is not simply a new technique or calculation. Like science, it is difficult to anticipate and can never be completely planned. It is a mental state, an impulse, a movement. It is a tracery of vision, energy, intuition and tentative moves. It fluctuates, hesitates, reconsiders, sweeps on. It cannot be completely classified. It is nourished by its own dynamism. It lights up, inspires, enriches itself from its successes and learns from its failures. It is constantly self-renewing. For the most part it is beyond analysis, theory or models. In essence, the process of innovation is fragile and can only develop if the internal and external environment is sufficiently favourable.

It cannot be stressed enough that this type of activity is very risky. There is a constant stream of innovations but not all will enjoy lasting success. The first off the starting blocks is not always the winner and acceptance by the market can vary enormously from case to case.

To take one example from hundreds, in 2000 the financial press announced with a great fanfare the largest merger ever – that between the internet world leader America On Line (AOL) and the media world leader Time-Warner'. This $164 billion operation represented a huge gamble on the convergence of a network with a supplier of contents such as films, radio, press and books. Three years later it was clear that the enterprise was failing, the partner businesses having lost 83 per cent of their stock market value at the time of the merger.

Other examples are the Vivendi adventure and the shipwreck of grand projects in the telecommunications sector, including Global Crossing, KPN Qwest and WorldCom. Numerous visions, dreams and strategies have been premature, overambitious or too complex. Some have stemmed from the 'triumph of hope over experience'.

If development through innovation is hazardous and risky, it is also brutal and dangerous because it is competitive (Lisbon Group, 1995). In the short term it can also have high social costs. Under the pressure of competition the firm is forced to adopt the logic of innovation, creativity and change. Long-term survival depends on the capacity to engage in the race for technical progress and to stay as long as possible at the forefront. In this regard the meaning of competition is explicit: to outrun the other. The terms used are: staying at the head of the field, being first off the starting blocks (prime mover), the race to the top, starting in prime position, racing ahead.

This incessant race enforces a culture of almost permanent change. The new is constantly substituted for the old, the past is more and more rapidly replaced by the future. The role that technological competition plays as a brutal accelerator never ceases to grow. Many firms, having become prosperous thanks to their mastery of a technology, decline or disappear upon the appearance of a new technology. Polaroid went bankrupt with the arrival of digital photography. Kodak was compelled to cut its workforce by 15 000 (20 per cent of the total) over three years as digital cameras reduced the demand for film. Apple lost part of its market because it was too slow to separate hardware from software. Pharmaceutical firms have survived or disappeared according to the pace of their innovations. The technology industry can be compared to a dinosaur in a world bombarded by meteorites such as the change from analogue to digital, which is breaking down the frontiers between consumer electronics, personal computers, the telephone and games, or the spread of broadband internet networks that provide direct access to information and entertainment.[5]

The race can be won by constantly cutting costs. That can take the form of relocation of activities and massive licensing. Competition is often merciless. Firms aim to supplant or destroy their rivals by advancing more rapidly on the technical, commercial or organizational front. Competition also has a bearing on the structure of sectors as firms combine to create groups that are powerful because of their size, resources and capacity for action. Jobs are destroyed as a result of the takeover or bankruptcy of the weakest firms. The struggle is

Darwinian in nature: the survival of the fittest, of the most capable. The language used is often that of war: big manoeuvres, field of battle, cut-throat competition, conquering bosses, the best-armed groups, the gateway war, strike force, competition with knives drawn, a blood bath in the high technologies, triumphant economy, the warrior using new arms, the DVD is killing the video cassette.[6]

Another striking example of this economic brutality is again provided by telecommunications. The deregulation of the sector was decided upon in a period of growth (1996). It unleashed competition in which technical advances have been transformed into innovations: mobile telephones have become ever more sophisticated, broadband has become accessible at the residential level, the use of the internet is constantly growing, and consumers have access to services that were unimaginable only ten years ago. Nonetheless the sector is experiencing great difficulties. The investment has been too rapid, consumer uptake has not followed the expected time scale, debt has mounted to an estimated $100 billion, 500 000 workers have lost their jobs, American firms have lost $2000 billion of their value on the stock exchange, and in Europe the loss is $700 billion.

The destructive effect of all this can be compared to that of an earthquake or a hurricane (Finkelstein, 2003). Progress has been made, but at a high cost. And firms do not have a choice. They are trapped in a competitive system that imposes on them the logic of movement, risk and innovation. The president of Sony has expressed this clearly: 'I believe that the mission of Sony is to make its own products out of date, if not, someone else will do it' (Nakamoto and Bort, 2003). At the same time he announced the loss of 20 000 jobs.

Marx also understood this logic: 'bourgeois capitalism can only survive through constantly revolutionizing the means of production' (Marx, 1848). Since the Middle Ages the development of capitalist trading has been carried out in the same spirit. The motto of the Hanseatic League was *Navigare necesse est*. Similarly Portuguese sailors discovering the world spoke of the need to take to the high seas: 'For the person who adjusts his sail properly to the breeze of progress, a new wind rises up that always forces him to take to the highest seas' (de Chardin, 1955).

The mechanism behind innovation and creative destruction has been the true engine of economic development in the West and elsewhere as it is powerful and has plenty of muscle. It is a question of 'ceaselessly renewed creation in a world destined to action' (Malraux, 1972). It has produced a level of economic growth unequalled in history. The firm is the central player and reflects the thousand-year effort of humans to improve their material circumstances. Since the mastery of fire and the invention of the first tools, the spirit of enterprise has pushed people to take risks and to innovate.

* * *

Today, enterprise is carried out in a world that has changed profoundly. The current trends are well known. This book will only consider those which touch firms the closest. Will they change firms' role, question their rationale or exacerbate it to the point of making it more ambiguous or even dangerous?

In the following chapters we shall examine three major topics: the acceleration of scientific and technical progress, the globalization of markets, and the absence of world governance and an ethic to promote the common good of the planet and guide the behaviour of economic players.

In the future firms are likely to pursue their strategies with new weapons, on a quite different scale and without any global regulation. All this will considerably increase their power of action and ambiguity unless their goals and values are clarified.

2
New Weapons: the Technosciences

The spirit of research is the permanent soul of evolution.

(Teilhard de Chardin)

If there is a prevailing trend in evolution it is that of science and the continual advance of knowledge over the centuries, whatever the vagaries of history and economic circumstances.

During the past century there have been unprecedented advances in the field of science. Several factors have contributed to this: the accumulation of knowledge and its rapid dissemination has opened up broader and more ambitious areas of investigation for researchers; the crossover of disciplines and universal access to information have encouraged new and more innovative lines of research; and the globalization of technological competition has expanded this movement and increased the funds devoted to research and development.[1] We have overcome many secrets that a few decades ago appeared unfathomable. For example we have established precise details of the origin of the universe and we now know about the 'music of the stars'. Christian de Duve, Nobel Prize winner for medicine, says enthusiastically:

Apart from its value as a source of new and beneficial technologies, basic research has proved an invaluable generator of knowledge and understanding. Almost within the span of a single century research has explained the nature of the universe, established the composition and history of matter, unravelled the most profound biological mechanisms, discovered the origin and evolution of

life on Earth, retraced the arrival of mankind and tackled the operation of his driving motor, the human brain. These are immensely
important historical events. It is thanks to them that we have
not only the unprecedented power to shape the future, but also
a completely transformed view of the world and our own nature.
(de Duve, 2002)

Since its first appearance, knowledge has been transformed into
technologies. Technical progress has always existed – ever since the
discovery of fire and invention of the wheel, humans have ceaselessly
tried to improve their material existence. What is new is the extraordinary expansion of research and the increasingly rapid transformation
of knowledge into concrete applications, thereby ensuring continual
technological progress. This phenomenon is known as technoscience,
and firms play an essential role in it. By mastering the methods and
tools of scientific rationalization they have been able to make use of
it in their economic strategies. Today they work in an environment
that strengthens their actions in a cumulative way by constantly
providing them with new opportunities and more powerful weapons.

Technoscience is therefore an element of economic power. Through
the vigorous driving force of firms, technological progress becomes
systematized, accelerates and spreads.

Systematization

By pursuing innovation, firms have institutionalized R&D activities,
thereby bringing about the systematization of technical progress.
They continually improve their ability to transform new knowledge
into profitable products and promote them on the market. Science
considerably increases their capacity for action and their economic
power. They allocate a substantial proportion of their budgets to R&D.
Expressed as a percentage of sales, R&D expenditure amounts to
about 5 per cent in the automotive industry, about 10 per cent in
telecommunications, 10–15 per cent in the software industry and
15–20 per cent in the pharmaceutical industry.

In absolute figures, these are significant sums. The top three car
manufacturers together spend nearly $20 billion on R&D. In 1999
the R&D budgets of pharmaceutical firms amounted to £2.9 billion
for Astra-Zeneca, £2.7 billion for Pfizer and $2.6 billion for Novartis.

Microsoft devoted $5.2 billion to R&D in 2003, which gave it a decisive advantage in the race for innovation. In answer to the question of how he might achieve market leadership similar to that of Windows in another field (for example mobile telephones), Bill Gates replied: 'My competitors cannot spend "zillions" of dollars. I am someone who can spend billions, five to be precise' (Martin and Gowers, 2001).

Firms go even further in the systematization of innovation. They try to put into practice theories such as that of Professor Nonaka: innovation is the key to winning strategies but its source lies in the ability to create and manage the knowledge of the whole enterprise (Nonaka and Hirotaka, 1995). This knowledge exists at every level in the organization. It may be explicit and easily transmittable, but it can also be tacit, unexpressed, locked in the 'tricks of the trade' or the reflex actions that arise from the daily practise of a task. Firms will become even more innovative if they succeed in explaining and generalizing these resources of knowledge, which until now have been little exploited (de Brabandère, 1998 and 2004).

One can see where the will to systematize the development of this intangible resource may lead. One can also see the advantage that dynamic firms can gain in this area.

Acceleration

Technical progress accelerates due to the effect of competition and the increasing funds that firms and public authorities devote to it. Recent studies have shown that the transition from invention (discovery) to commercial exploitation took 112 years for photography, 56 years for the telephone, 35 years for radio, 15 years for radar, 12 years for television, six years for the atomic bomb, five years for transistors, three years for solar batteries and a few months for the new generations of electronic components. 'In less than 10 years, the Internet has succeeded in bringing together as many users as television has achieved in 50 years and radio in more than a century' (Salvaggio and Callis, 2002).

One of the most significant results of this acceleration is the shortening of product life. In the chemical sector, for example, it is not unusual for large firms to renew almost half of their range of products in less than ten years. In the pharmaceutical sector the average life of a special drug is rarely more than four years. In some cases progress is radical, for example human insulin produced by means of cultured cells is better than that produced from the pancreatic glands of millions of pigs (Zizi, 2003).

The rate of technical progress is clearly visible in the world of computers, digital photography and mobile telephones. In 50 years the capacity of electronic memories has multiplied by a million – from one megabyte (a million) in 1952 to one terabyte (a million million) in 2002. As for transmission networks, these have multiplied and continued to increase in capacity and speed:[2] cable, optical fibres, satellites, asychronous transmission (ADSL), high delivery rate (VDSL and XDSL) and third-generation mobile telephones. This has opened the way for the development of a variety of on-demand services, such as time-shifted television and on-demand video.

Equally important for research, defence, geophysics, meteorology and encryption, processing power continues to grow. The supercomputer made by the Japanese firm NEC, Earth Simulator, is capable of producing 35 600 billion calculations per second (gigaflops), whereas its predecessor, Hewlett-Packard's most advanced machine at Los Alamos, only manages 7724 billion. In this sector the race involves gigantic investments, for example $20 billion for the IBM supercomputer Aski Purple.

Generalization

One might imagine that technical progress only affects the so-called 'scientific' sectors, but this is not the case. Other long-established sectors have become aware of the importance of research and they too systematically carry it out in order to improve their methods, products and productivity. Such is the case with the financial and insurance sectors, which continually launch new products, not least of which is the bank card. The same applies to heavy industries such as glass, construction materials and steel. Large glass manufacturers such as Saint Gobain and Asahi are constantly innovating and base their strategies on the creation of higher added value products, such as reflecting, filtering and toughened glass for buildings and cars.

By devoting 3 per cent of its turnover to research, the cosmetics industry has created an advanced sector known as cosmeceutical, which has brought the industry closer to the pharmaceutical sector and allowed it to sell 'eternal youth'. In the field of construction materials, Lafarge has launched products such as self-locating concrete blocks, which shorten construction times, and high-performance, fibre-reinforced concrete, which is highly durable and able to flex.

This general spreading of technical progress often occurs when new technological families or 'clusters' of disciplines emerge. The metatechnologies are making a powerful contribution to the spread of technical advancement. They control the development of a wide variety of sectors and drive them to innovate and transform themselves. In this respect the conquest of space speaks for itself: space has stimulated thousands of enterprises in areas as important and diverse as aeronautics, communications, launchers, instruments for researching, navigating and observing the Earth, satellites, and physical, chemical and alimental equipment for manned flight.

The internet is another example. It was thought that this would be dominated by the new enterprises (dot coms) of a new economy that would gradually replace the old economy. But older firms have also moved onto the internet, chiefly those engaged in commerce and services. Currently 87 per cent of British firms use e-business technology to improve their performance. American consumers spend tens of billions of dollars on on-line commerce, representing an important source of productivity gains for that country.

Although the biotechnology revolution has only just begun (Zizi, 2003), it will affect most economic sectors as soon as tools are developed to manipulate genes. Its impact will quickly be felt in biomedicine, the food-processing industry, material science and chemistry.

These fields of activity have become major factors in the development of nation-states, improving their competitiveness, military power and degree of independence. This is why they receive substantial public funds. The latter are more than mere economic stakes as they provide real support for the strategies of enterprises, even though this often distorts the conditions for competition.

The new scientific clusters contribute greatly to the spread of technical advancement and offer vast opportunities for enterprises. The European Commission, in its sixth research programme framework 2002–6, will support seven priority areas:

- Life sciences, genomics and health biotechnologies.
- Information technologies.
- Nanotechnologies and nanosciences, 'intelligent' multifunctional materials, new production techniques.

- Aeronautics and space research.
- The quality and safety of food production.
- Sustainable development, global change and ecosystems.
- Governance and citizenship in a knowledge society.

The new technological clusters, enlarged areas of activity and the spread of progress have necessitated the restructuring of several industries, which in order to choose the best option have allied themselves with other sectors, diversified their operations and embarked on mergers or acquisitions that would have appeared absurd before the appearance of these new activities.

There has been an increase in the number of giant corporations with multiple but complementary activities. This is clearly the case in the media world, which has close ties with the network and internet sector. The expansion of News Corporation (owned by Rupert Murdoch) stems from a multisectoral approach of this type, as did the disappointing purchase of Time-Warner (films, newspapers, music, TV and so on) by AOL (networks).

Convergence and integration in the field of information and communication has driven many firms to raise their operations to the highest technological level. There has also been a re-examination of the stand-alone strategy by firms, even if they are 'national champions'. The 'digital battlefield' is based on technological capacity and necessitates mergers and large-scale cooperative ventures.

We should add that such strategies create new value chains. In telecommunications, for example, the chain consists of equipment manufacturers, software and components producers, operators, service providers, distributors and consumers. The principle of the value chain is to raise each link to the same technical level, and this acts as a powerful engine for advancement. This phenomenon occurs in many sectors, including the automotive industry (just-in-time production), aeronautics and space, distribution, new materials and so on.

The rapid spread of innovations is also a result of licensing. In the pharmaceutical industry, for example, 24 per cent of the turnover of the 20 largest firms is accounted for by products licensed by other firms, which in the majority of cases are innovative small and medium-sized enterprises. Many of the best-selling drugs are the product of partnerships between a small but innovative firm and a large company endowed with commercial strength (Firn, 2003).

The 'open standard' practice allows other firms, often competitors, to take up an innovation and transform it into a technological benchmark for the rest of the industry. The ultimate outcome of this is the adoption of a standard by a large number of manufacturers, if not all. There have been famous battles for supremacy in this area: in European TV there was a battle between PAL and SECAM; in video recorders the fact that Panasonic made its VHS system freely available enabled it to establish the system as the world standard in the face of Sony's technically superior Betacam; the same situation occurred with Windows and Apple in the software field; and in mobile telephony there is currently a struggle between Symbian (for equipment manufacturers) and Smartphone-Microsoft (for operators).

In this race for advancement firms have adopted the resources of science and technology and turned them into a decisive competitive weapon, thus strengthening and systematizing their innovative function. Never before have they played their Promethean role so creatively. 'Listen rather to the miseries of mortal beings and what I have done for these weak creatures that I have led to Reason and to the power of Thought . . .'

Science and technology have changed the life of human beings and they will doubtless honour many of the extraordinary promises they are offering today. But their advancement presents new and difficult problems that may have major consequences for society and its future. Obviously any responsible firm must take this into account. One of these problems is the ambiguous nature of technology and the applications of science.

Ambiguity

Technical progress can be beneficial or harmful, depending on the use made of it. More than ever it must be remembered that technology is only a means, and not an end in itself. This brings us to the ethical dimension at the heart of this book. A few examples should suffice to illustrate this.

Genetic engineering promises abundant harvests, the healing of incurable diseases, the prolonging of our life, the retardation of degeneration and so on. However it also raises the spectre of genetic manipulation producing unforeseeable consequences, touching the very nature of humanity and all other species. Jean-Claude Guillebaud (2002) has rung an alarm bell by showing the serious threats that science, and in particular the biosciences, pose for humanity. For example brain research may irreversibly transform the nature of humanity.

In biological matters, practically everything is of dual purpose: to protect or destroy life. Should this type of research therefore be forbidden? Should we limit 'technology transfers aimed at helping numerous countries equip themselves with the necessary knowledge for the creation and maintenance of health and medical conditions similar to those in the industrialized world?' (Zizi, 2003). Should we further increase our control over the applications of science by, for example, regulating the terms of the political debate on the essential questions it raises?

Nuclear technology can detect illnesses, cure some cancers and protect food, the mail and medical instruments from contamination. It provides cheap energy without polluting the atmosphere, but its waste poses a long-term threat. Nuclear weapons can be effective instruments of deterrence in the hands of responsible governments, but a means of blackmail and terror in the hands of extremists or rogue states.

The internet and other media offer unlimited prospects in terms of information exchange, interactive communication, debate and education. This might create the 'noosphere' that is so dear to Teilhard de Chardin (1955) and facilitate the advent of a world unified in its diversity. But they also carry with them all the disadvantages of information overload, simplification, confinement within narrow specializations and identity fantasies. They may also magnify on a world scale the threats to security, the growth of mafia networks, the spread of images of violence or pornography and so on. Moreover they oblige us to rethink certain concepts, such as the protection of privacy, which is already threatened by the commercialization of personal data in the interests of marketing (Tabatoni, 2000–3).

Another problem is the autonomy enjoyed by the technosciences. George Steiner (1973) has described this well. In contrast to art, science works through accumulation and its development is exponential. In the meantime it avoids democratic debate. The technosciences have acquired their own dynamism and independence and run the risk of following dangerous paths.

Every definition of a civilization coming after classicism must learn to reckon with scientific knowledge and with the universe of mathematical and symbolic languages. For they alone are all powerful: both factually as well as in the fever of progress that characterises us.... It falls within the meaning that science and technology have brought about irreparable damage to the environment, economic imbalance and moral laxity...

However, despite the confused and naive criticisms of writers such as Thoreau and Tolstoy, no one has seriously doubted that this path had to be followed. There is in this attitude, generally irrational, an element of blind mercantile instinct, an excessive thirst for comfort and consumption. But also a much more powerful mechanism: the conviction, rooted in the heart of the Western personality, at least since Grecian times, that intellectual investigation must go forward, that such an impulse is natural and commendable in itself, that man is devoted to the pursuit of truth. (Steiner, 1973)

The third problem, which is linked to the others, is that science and technology have advanced faster than political, legal and ethical thinking, and they have posed new questions that have taken us completely by surprise. This explains people's mistrust of genetically modified crops, genetic engineering and nuclear energy, as well as the current debates on the status of embryos and the protection of privacy in the information society. Researchers who have a role in the democratic debate are not prepared for these new challenges.

What must be underlined here is the danger we shall face if we delay integrating scientific and technical progress into an ethical and political vision of the future of the planet, if we leave the technosciences to follow their own dynamic and the logic of the market.

There is the temptation to regard the advancement of science and technology as an end in itself. The naïve belief that scientific knowledge and the mastery of nature are the keys to human progress is still too prevalent among many experts, economists and business leaders. One only has to listen to scientists who have ventured outside their fields to be convinced that their discipline provides them with no special ability in matters of politics or ethics. We must cease believing that science can by itself provide the direction for the future. It restricts itself to the advancement of knowledge, but even here its methods limit it to the positive, measurable and reproducible knowledge that constitute its greatness.

Neither mankind nor society can be reduced to the scientific approach. Human components may be dissected in the interests of research, but people's mystery, freedom, loves and beliefs are of a different order. As for society, it can only be democratically organized on the basis of fragile and continually renewed compromises that stem not from science but from politics; we should remember that politics is a science of which one can never become a doctor.

The ambiguity of the demiurgic power of science and technology shows its full relevance in the spread of weapons of mass destruction and international terrorism, the unauthorized cloning of human beings and so on. We should never forget the barbarisms of the twentieth century. Can history still be regarded as a march forward? Can one still speak of an automatic link between the progress of science and that of mankind? Can we speak of progress 'as though Auschwitz had never existed' (Gesché, 1993)?

Science and those who use it must be subject to the common good. They cannot dictate the important choices of society, even if they can shed light on them and allow them to be implemented. Rabelais anticipated this when he warned that 'science without conscience is no more than loss of the soul'.

It is from the standpoint of ethics and politics that we should seek the values and orientation of our development. This must be done with the vigour that, in the long term, is found in true democracies, and also with the patience and modesty that is necessary in human affairs.

3

New Spaces: Globalization of the Market Economy

> *When we wander at full sail on this sea and we believe that sea and stars are for us.*
>
> (La Fontaine)

Opening up and growing interdependence

Since Neolithic times humans have striven to improve their material circumstances by gathering resources, inventing tools and expanding trade. As soon as surpluses could be generated, trade became one of the most powerful engines of economic development. Commerce developed, money was invented, competition emerged. Since then the markets have never ceased to put the economy under pressure, thus causing long lasting development trends.

Braudel (1979) has shown the time it took for the West to construct these complex mechanisms, which are effective but often fragile. The journey from the first fairs in Champagne to the markets for options and derivatives has been long, adventurous and inventive. Along with technology, the market was the source of material progress and cultural and social evolution. 'The Venetians are traders but what genius does it require to transform salt and dried fish into spices and silks and the latter into Giorgione and Palladio' (Tristan, 1984).

These mechanisms will drive the globalization that is accelerating before our eyes and in which enterprises are the chief players. The large commercial chains were almost always international but the global integration of commerce, industry and finance only began in the nineteenth century within the framework of the Industrial

Revolution and European colonialism. This was interrupted by the two world wars and the great depression, only to resume later on a broader base.

Economic globalization is a vast and complex topic that is widely debated and often demonized or glorified, to the detriment of more serious analysis. Under the influence of liberal thinking, the opening up of markets, deregulation and privatization have created room for free trade that continues to expand. Means of communication have advanced astonishingly and provided us with flexible global networks that facilitate increasingly rapid responses. Financial markets and tools also become global and the availability of finance has burgeoned.

These developments have fostered new trade and investment. Enterprising and innovative players have moved onto the stage, and with them competition has expanded throughout the world. Enterprises regard this as an opportunity rather than a threat – caught up in a movement that appears irreversible, they have decided to lead it instead of being subject to it.

Such initiatives are creating an economy that is capable of functioning as a unit, in real time, on a global scale (Castells, 1998). The elements of this economy are interdependent and enterprises adopt integrated strategies that ensure global coherence of their activities. The elements of their value chain (the important functions of research, production, distribution and so on) and supply chain (suppliers, subcontractors, transporters and so on) are often situated in many countries and involve a true policy of integration.

In the industrialized countries the average customs charge has progressively fallen from 40 per cent to 5 per cent. International commerce has multiplied by 15 in 50 years.[1] Mergers and cross-border acquisitions have continued to increase, rising from $336 billion in 1988 to $544 billion in 1998. Direct foreign investment has also followed this trend, rising fivefold in less than ten years (1990–99). Over the same period the flow of private funds abroad was six times greater than the flow of public funds.

In short, the entire developed economy is caught up in a trend towards internationalization and integration that continues to grow.

This phenomenon is most visible in high-technology sectors with high added value, such as communications, state-of-the-art chemistry, space, and so on. However this is not new. Since the distant past international commerce has seized upon the highest value activities

(Braudel, 1979). Today, software, drugs and aeroplanes have simply replaced spices and silks.

What is new is that the majority of other sectors have also been gripped by globalization. Whether one thinks of restructuring in the metallurgical industries, the leisure industry, consumer goods such as McDonald's and Coca Cola, agriculture and oil shipping, one can see that strategies have become global in almost all sectors.

This transformation has also occurred in the financial sector, in a even faster and more general way.

The liberalization of capital markets has allowed financial players that are often dynamic and creative, and sometimes speculative (the 'casino' economy), to cover the world with their networks and offer their most sophisticated products around the world, around the clock.

Capital movements, both private and public, for the short, medium or long term, have being growing for several decades and the aim of financial companies is to respond immediately to the demand for credit or capital, no matter where or when, day in and day out.

Investments abroad encourage even deeper integration than does commerce. In 2000 American and European companies held $8800 billion of assets in each other's territory. The turnover of their subsidiaries totalled $2200 billion, that is, four times the value of bilateral commerce. They employed 8.5 million staff (de Jonquières, 2003a).

The free circulation of capital means that it is more readily available for profitable projects and enterprises. This facilitates international investment, but also short-term speculative capital movements that may create instability and generate crises.

It also increases the power of financial capitalism. The ownership of enterprises is falling increasingly into the hands of large investment houses and pension funds. The latter manage savings and private funds without intervening in the management of the companies, except through the stock markets. Their decision-making criteria are mainly if not exclusively financial. They help to make economic activities increasingly financial by championing the single criterion of shareholder value. Often their influence is overwhelming and it is no accident that opponents of globalization refer to them as 'the new rulers of the world'.

The new trend is therefore the opening up of markets, leading to the globalization of trade, finance and strategic decision-making. Such decisions are now made in an integrated way, taking a global view of the system rather than splitting it up by country or activity.

What is also new in the phenomenon of globalization is that it is partially beyond the control and legislation of nation-states. Global economic space has been occupied by enterprises and financiers without new rules of the game being completely established.

The negative aspects of globalization will be examined later, but it is important to note here the extent to which the increase in trade contributes to the economic development and technical progress of those countries which master the mechanisms. The market dynamic has made a large contribution to the creation of wealth. If one only considers the economic aspect, global production is nowadays 50 times more than it was in 1820, whereas the population has only risen sixfold.

For a long time the market was regarded as an element of civilization. In the early days it took the place of pillage by establishing relationships based on dialogue, reason, interest and the acceptance of differences. It was also the driving force behind the spirit of enterprise and technical creativity. By placing the economic players in competition, the market encouraged competitiveness and a race for material advancement. It took several centuries for the West to put into place the mechanisms and structures of trade. These resulted from the fundamental transformation of institutions, know-how and behaviour. They opened up societies, raised standards of living and encouraged innovation.

This opening up, the spirit of enterprise and market competition are clearly the sources of economic development and wealth creation, and they should be integrated into our analyses and policies in order to preserve the positive aspects of them. If we speak in terms of effectiveness, productivity or creativity, the superiority of the market economy over the controlled economy is beyond question.

It is worth recording here the views of one of the most perceptive critics of the evolution of societies, J. C. Guillebaud. His questioning does not relate to the effectiveness of the market, but – as the present book suggests – to the aims and values that guide its development:

> The market has brought us more beneficial effects than it has generated barbarism. In a general way, it has even been a constituent

of Western progress whereas the societies that objected to its logic were condemned to stagnation and tyranny. All of that is beyond debate, as is the unequalled effectiveness of the market economy. From this point of view, the so-called 'debates' about the compared advantages of the controlled economy have become laughable. Do we still debate about whether the Earth is round? (Guillebaud, 1999).

The enterprise: a global player and private power

Today the most dynamic players in globalization are enterprises (industry, services, finance) and those who control them (investment funds). They were the first to adapt to this phenomenon and have quickly developed an effective and efficient international know-how that allows them to exploit it systematically.

In fact enterprises are among the few organizations that have succeeded in simultaneously crossing all the thresholds of globalization:

- The *size* threshold: many of them are multinationals and transcend the frontiers of the nation-state.
- The *time horizon* threshold: they pursue long-term strategies on a different scale to those in the political, administrative or educational world.
- The *complexity* threshold: they have become capable of managing cultural diversity, multiple rationality, international risks; they are also capable of change and rapid adaptation.
- The *resource and information* threshold: This allows them to be 'plugged into' the world and react effectively and promptly.

Because of their competitive dynamism and spirit of enterprise, companies adapt more quickly to globalization than the majority of other institutions, be they political, social, legal and so on.

In a famous article Theodore Levitt wrote: 'The world's needs and desires have been irrevocably homogenized. This makes the multinational corporation obsolete and the global enterprise absolute.'[2] In the case of certain companies this assertion is true. For example Coca Cola and McDonald's have become the very symbols of globalization. The same goes for Walt Disney, MTV, Pepsi, Fuji, Kodak and so on. But the reality is more complex since the current slogan is to 'think globally and act locally'. This assumes a huge ability to adapt and differentiate.

As already noted the high technology sectors have, by nature, an international vocation. But even in the more traditional sectors the same is beginning to apply, and for many industries globalization is becoming a necessity. When a company begins to raise itself to the global level its competitors are often obliged to follow it, and when it becomes truly international, not only its competitors but also some of its suppliers must do so too. The automotive industry provides a good example: manufacturers of tyres, glass, steel and components have been compelled to become more international in order to supply the large car manufacturers wherever they are located. In turn the suppliers of these subcontractors have had to follow suit, for example the producers of cord for radial tyres have developed on a world scale, and so it goes on. The pressure to train up is felt in a growing number of activities. When prospects or opportunities expand, companies tend to raise their strategic capacity to a level that will allow them to remain competitive.

We should underline here that there is a constraint that the market economy system imposes on the company: the latter is inserted into a growth model that it drives but which compels it to match the pace. In order to do this, companies create and develop their global reach and their power of action.

Liberal ideologists are quickly irritated when the power of the company is evoked. One can understand this when it involves superficial remarks by naïve anti-internationalists who contrast the turnover of General Motors with the gross national product of the poorest countries. One can understand it less when it involves more serious studies that tell us about control of the key resources of the economic initiative and the ability to conduct global strategies.

Resource strategy and strategic capacity

In order to respond to the challenge of globalization, companies have to develop a more global strategic capacity. Merely, having sufficient capital or financial reserves is not enough. Rather it is necessary to develop all the qualitative attributes that permit collective action on a grand scale. It is from this point of view that companies pursue a resource strategy.

The permanent possession and development of key resources for performance and international competitiveness is a precondition for their survival. That is why they collect and develop scientific and technical knowledge, management and organizational skills, teams of high-grade executives and managers, and all types of relationship: social, political, financial and so on.

They also attempt to create a culture of change and learning that enables them to remain in the race rather than fall behind.

Their policy for the development of human resources focuses on permanent improvement, not only of knowledge but also of know-how and 'knowing how to be': teamwork, communication, leadership . . . An important new practice in recent years has been to turn the company into a learning organization in order better to handle complexity, new technologies and market evolution.

These resources arm the company for world-wide competitive battles. They also enable it to react more quickly to the rapidly changing environment and to be less vulnerable to surprises and breakdowns. The acceleration of scientific progress and the globalization of competitive interplay make the world very uncertain and even less predictable than before. As Paul Valéry (1988) says, 'alas, the future is no longer just as it used to be'. Companies have understood that when little can be foreseen they must prepare themselves to be ready for anything and be quick to react. This is why a resource strategy is increasingly being added to forecasting and planning, which have been rendered inadequate in such a rapidly changing environment. Successful companies even tend to overprovide themselves with key resources for their development. They allow themselves flexibility, a comfort margin, a slack that facilitates action and continual trans-formation.[3] This is one of the current methods of operation favoured by the entrepreneur. Such companies therefore possesses strategic reserves that allow them to seize new opportunities and rid themselves of bad risks.

Productivity and cost reduction remain an important competitive weapon, but this often involves a defensive stance. When taken too far, cost reduction, particularly in relation to activities aimed at preparing for the future, such as training or research, may make the company incapable of movement.

Strategic manoeuvres require a capacity for action and innovation, which can only be provided by reserves of key resources. However, as we shall see later, it is precisely this capacity for creating and orienting key resources of development that causes ambiguity in a poorly regulated system when it is applied at the global level.

Strategy of external growth

As the competitive interplay has grown in scale, the enlargement of the strategic and capacities of the company becomes a condition of its performance, and even of its survival. The result is a race for leadership and the fastest strategy is often that of external growth. The practice of strategic acquisitions and alliances spread widely in the 1980s and 1990s. It was rooted in the will to achieve sufficient economic and financial power to survive. If the stock market was sufficiently buoyant 'the possibility for investing and buying is practically unlimited'.[4]

These decades witnessed a series of moves towards links and alliances among companies with a view to adapting to the new global game. The first wave of mergers and acquisitions in the 1980s were mainly carried out by ambitious managers or financiers who were more sensitive to size or short-term financial value than to the problems of strategy and organization. The majority of these acquisitions were hostile. They often led to excessive diversification, insurmountable management problems and unexpected break-ups. Being more financial than strategic, they produced few results in terms of long-term performance. From the point of view of shareholders, those with shares in the acquiring company generally suffered a loss in the value of their shares (Auerbach, 1989).

The 1990s saw the second major wave of mergers and acquisitions. These were often 'friendly' and based on a more systematic vision of long-term development and of new strategies to be pursued. Some will doubtless result in the creation of successful global enterprises that will occupy the top of the pyramid for a while. Whether they will cause a significant reduction in competition is too soon to say, although current statistics do not seem to indicate that they will. The most we can say is that there are oligopolies in certain segments, but in the new industries the pace of technical progress and the strength of competition are such that dominant positions are quickly challenged.

The same goes for alliances and cooperative ventures in which several areas of activity are combined. For example the digital revolution has considerably stepped up convergence in the IT, telecommunication and media sectors. The alliance that links Microsoft, Intel and Sony is a good illustration of this. Another example is the consortium that produces Airbus.

The power of large companies is not simply due to their size – they continue to rely on their creativity and entrepreneurial qualities. We should not underestimate the difficulties of external growth, and it is vital not to confuse size with performance. Economies of scale are only one aspect of the competitive game since they only affect the control of costs. The same goes for market power and the global dimension. Although these are no doubt necessary preconditions for international success, they are not enough to ensure the achievement and maintenance of decisive comparative advantage. Size is insufficient in the face of technological competition and multifaceted creativity by entrepreneurs. In this respect the example of IBM is interesting. Twenty years ago the American authorities were concerned about IBM's commercial and technical domination of the world of computers. Today the game has moved on to software and the market capitalization of Microsoft is twice that of IBM's.

Innovation, creative initiative and the spirit of enterprise will remain the keys to economic success. Mergers and acquisitions only lead to success if they strengthen the creative process of competitiveness discussed later. The company's strategic capacity is based on the ability to anticipate, develop key resources and respond speedily to challenges and opportunities. These factors depend more on quality than on quantity: large size often causes bureaucracy and slowness. Extremely large research laboratories are only effective when work is conducted in small teams, innovators are stifled by vast structures, customer service does not really exist unless it is personalized, and so on.

This amounts to saying that the pursuit of size, in itself, cannot be a winning strategy. What makes companies win is their ability to raise their creativity to the global level. They must be able to define and share their strategic vision, control complex structures, motivate their staff and customers, and detect the paradoxes and uncertainties of a more difficult and more dangerous competitive game. Simply wanting to create an empire does not constitute a strategy. It is enough to consider the fate of the merger of AOL and Time-Warner and the grand design of Vivendi to appreciate this.

Many join the game and find themselves drawn into situations that are beyond them. For them, competitive battles are based not exclusively on reason but also on passion, the passion to win. At the time of the AOL – Time Warner merger the boss of one of the companies told the press that he was just as excited as on the night 42 years earlier when he had first made love.[5]

That said, when they are conducted well, acquisitions and alliances can considerably strengthen companies' power in the global arena. There are many examples of this, including the merger of pharmaceutical companies to form the giants of research and distribution: Aventis, Pfizer, Astra-Zeneca, Smithkline-Beecham and Glaxo-Wellcome, becoming GSK. Each of these companies spends $2–3 billion on research and development and have raised themselves to the peak of global competition.

One could also cite cement, iron and steel production, aeronautics, household equipment and airline transport, not to mention media and communications: Rupert Murdoch is pursuing a worldwide satellite platform, and by buying Direct TV he will round off his network with the top channel in the US and its 10 million subscribers.

Mergers and regroupings of companies may also be brought about by the politics of states. Defence policies are an illustration. Public spending on military equipment is four times higher in the US than the combined spending of the UK, France, Germany and Italy. European companies risk irretrievable backwardness if they do not elevate themselves to the level of their American competitors. They can only do this through cooperation or merger, as in the case of Airbus.

The growing desire to increase the economic power of Europe is driving governments and companies to form large groups such as EADS[6] for space and military projects. For example discussions are being held on grouping naval construction companies together to create a maritime EADS. The decision to launch the Galileo project, the European GPS (Global Positioning by Satellite), is in the same vein.

Cumulative process of competitiveness: an inescapable game

In their race for market share, many companies have had to raise their capacity for strategic action to the international level. To achieve this they have embarked on a cumulative process of competitiveness. This process is ongoing and they will have to remain competitive in this new space or disappear. Since their criteria for decision making are economic, commercial and financial, the process may lead to major ambiguities and pose questions of a political nature. We shall return to this later.

In Europe, research into this development has revealed its dynamic aspects and its obligatory, not to say inevitable character (de Woot, 1990). International competition draws the company into a commercial, technological or political environment that exerts a decisive influence on the opportunities and threats it must confront. But this environment is also strongly driven by the company itself, which plays a central and often innovatory role in it by changing the balance of power and constantly stirring up the competitive game by means of strategic initiatives. For companies of a certain size the process is based on the following elements:

- *Good long-term prospects* and sufficiently large opportunities to justify the risks; these opportunities may be offered by the opening up of markets, rapidly growing demand, new technologies, public projects and so on.
- Creating an *adequate strategic capacity* to operate on an international scale: this is the policy of creating and orienting resources discussed earlier.
- The possession of *competitive advantage at the international level*: with this capacity the company can achieve superiority in terms of products, prices or customer services, as well as having the possibility of playing on the differences between countries, benefiting from their comparative advantages and adapting quickly to their development. It also acquires a size that brings it economies of scale and a cost advantage that may be decisive for many activities. It benefits from the experiences gained from the combined advantages of learning, size and innovation. It creates for itself sufficient synergies between activities and resources to optimize intangible investments such as research, marketing, management and so on.
- *Sufficient profitability* to cover the costs of development and internationalization, as well as the risks of its more daring manoeuvres. It goes without saying that the profitability of current operations (a sound core-business) is constantly monitored and maintained at the level required by the demands of the market and competition. Adaptations are made on an ongoing basis rather than in response to crises. Profitability allows advantage to be taken of opportunities that arise in the external environment and improves prospects for

the distant future. The virtuous loop is therefore closed and the process becomes dynamically competitive.

Here we have a logic that requires the company always to ride the highest wave, to maintain its competitive advantages at the international level and not to make any concessions on the conditions of its performance. Obviously this is complex, difficult and delicate. It depends on the quality of information available and the methods of management used, and also on the personal qualities of the managers and good leadership at every level of the organization. These must be attended to if the mechanisms of wealth creation are to be preserved or replaced when necessary. If the company does not follow this logic it runs the risk of failing.

The same research shows that less successful companies are caught up in a destructive competitive process. If the prospects are too short term and the opportunities too local, strategic capacity is not developed sufficiently and international comparative advantages cannot be created. Profitability suffers and there are insufficient financial resources to take action, adapt to changing circumstances and seize future opportunities.

The globalization of markets leaves companies with no choice: they must play the competitive game to the end or go under. This is the mechanism that underlies strategies and obliges companies to raise themselves to the world level. This process gives our development model a cumulative and inevitable character. At the heart of this a *power* for action is systematically built and continues to grow. This is true for both companies and states, as we shall see later.

What must be stressed is that the company of today is capable of operating on a world scale, thanks to its mastery of strategic resources that give it great power. Extremely large-scale projects can be undertaken. 'At present, the media companies exchange agreements that are like those concluded by nation-states. They are simply more complex, more subtle and more flexible.'[7] This statement, made by the head of AOL at the time of ending the alliance with Bertelsmann in order to approach Time-Warner, illustrates this point in a quite arrogant way.

The company's power to act is based not only on its capital or financial strength but also on a set of tangible and intangible resources, such as knowledge, know-how, relationship networks and the capacity to manage complexity, uncertainty and paradox. It is thanks to flexibility, learning, creativity, leadership at every level and a culture of questioning, opening up and innovating that the successful company has been able to take advantage of the new space opened up by globalization.

4
New Power: Political Deficit and Ethical Vacuum

Feudal anarchy is nothing more than despotism brought together on many heads.

(Mirabeau)

A poorly governed world

Economic globalization is advancing much faster than world governance. It is escaping from the nation-state and progressively imposing its logic on the entire planet. This gap between the political and the economic is causing public powerlessness in respect of pursuing proper development strategies and democratically debating the societal stakes of globalization.

It is as though globalization is imposing itself on nation states, leaving them not even the freedom to choose the type of market economy that suits them best. Hence the Anglo-Saxon model, which is more financial than social, is striving to gain ground over a more human model, such as the social market or Rhineland model (Albert, 1991). We recall here the continual pressure that the Anglo-Saxon countries exert on Western Europe to reform its structures, which is necessary up to a point but in spirit indicates at least a partial breaking up of social security systems.

Since there is little global regulation of an economic game that is forever expanding, people are beginning to lose their political reference points. They feel that their jobs, life styles, social security and cultural identity are being threatened.

This is the result of two major facts. The first is to do with a dominant ideology that is tending to become a single thought: the globalization movement is underpinned by a set of simplistic and limited concepts that are directed too exclusively at trusting the market to develop the planet. The second concerns the powerlessness of states to define the world's common good. They clearly do not have a suitable political and legal framework to direct and regulate globalization.

Single thought: a simplistic and instrumental ideology

The more an ideology dominates, the weaker the political debate. When the related thinking becomes unique, democracy runs the risk of becoming purely formal. Clothed in the respectability of the dynamism and efficiency of a world opened up to trade, globalization conceals a radical ideology. Putting it simply, it is a question of too absolute a faith in the efficiency of markets and an almost visceral mistrust of public intervention and regulations. The globalization movement is imposing its logic throughout the world without taking sufficient account of political, cultural and institutional differences, somewhat in the manner of a roadroller. Everyone knows that the market economy is a successful growth model, but pushed to its limits the model may become an ideology.

For a long time the market ideology has had many supporters. It rules in the US and UK; it is accepted in continental Europe; it has been adopted to varying degrees by several Asian countries. Some of the larger international institutions attempt to impose it on the whole world. In the West it still appeals to the majority of business leaders and management schools. It is the greatest barrier to the emergence of truly responsible firms.

Its power of conviction is based on a simplified explanation of its internal logic, but also on an element of truth it contains: continued growth of the countries that, thanks to their historical advancement, have been able to gain from this system.

Simplifying greatly, one can summarise the dominant ideology as follows:

- The *market economy* is the most effective system for the creation of wealth; other systems have shown their inability to respond to the needs of creditworthy consumers in a flexible and dynamic way.

- The central driving force of this system is *competition*. This encourages innovation; it ensures the best division of work according to the comparative advantages of the countries in question; it exerts constant pressure on prices, to the great advantage of consumers.
- *Free trade* encourages growth; any barrier to trade – customs duties, subsidies, various protective measures – can only reduce the effectiveness of the market.
- Markets are efficient; they operate like an *invisible hand* to ensure the best allocation of resources.
- *Profit* is the unique criterion of performance; it guarantees growth, innovation, the securing of markets; it also ensures future financing because shareholders are satisfied.
- *Financial orthodoxy* encourages the smooth running of the system; rigorous monetary and budgetary policies and balanced accounts guarantee price stability and monetary strength.
- The market economy goes hand in hand with *freedom, democracy and peace* and may even encourage these in places where they do not yet exist; in company with science and technology, it ensures continued progress for humanity and therefore serves the general interest and the common good.[1]

This clearly indicates the direction of development and progress for humanity. It even proclaims the 'end of history' in a reconciled, prosperous and democratic world (Fukuyama, 1992).

Such an ideology thus attempts to elevate the game of the market from the level of means to that of ends. It ignores the fact that economic progress does not constitute the whole of human progress, even if it is a condition of it, and that it must be subject to the ethical and political imperatives that express the common good. It also seems to ignore that the latter is not yet defined at the global level and that there are few political or legal authorities sufficiently capable or caring to do it.

It also forgets that private economic players have considerable control of the planet's resources, the orientation of those resources and the type of development pursued.

It scarcely pays attention to the dangers of allowing economic power to expand in a poorly regulated space in which there is a risk of the law of the strongest prevailing. This is but a step away from suggesting that this single thought is used as an instrument of power in the market.

We should mention in passing the hypocrisy of Western political leaders and certain sectorial lobbies who wish to impose this model on the entire world but refuse to apply it themselves when it does not work in their favour.

As for the responsibilities of the firm, the following is what Milton Friedman (1970) said on the matter and has been taken up by virtually all management schools:

> The social responsibility of the firm is to increase its profits. When leaders state that the firm must have a social conscience and take seriously its responsibilities in matters of employment, discrimination, environment or anything that may have crossed the mind of the reformers, they are in fact preaching a pure and raw socialism... In a system of free enterprise and private ownership, the top manager is the employee of the shareholders... His responsibility is to conduct the firm according to their wishes and this is normally to make as much money as possible while respecting the basic rules of society in legal matters and current practice in ethical matters.

As we know, the theoretical foundations of this concept were proposed by a number of brilliant economists (the Chicago School, the new economists and so on) who had a considerable influence on strong political personalities, such as Ronald Reagan and Margaret Thatcher. The latter caused the theories to spread throughout the world by promoting the move towards trade liberalization, deregulation and privatization that has characterized globalization.

This ideology also guides the majority of important economic decisions taken by international organizations such as the International Monetary Fund, the World Bank, and the World Trade Organization. It also influenced the famous Washington Consensus, which has been described by the financier George Soros as market fundamentalism (*Financial Times*, 3 August 2003). The will to privatize everything that can be privatized is starting to bear on public services such as the mail, social security and even prisons and some military activities.[2]

By placing a strong emphasis on economics, this approach secured the following of the majority of Anglo-Saxon business leaders, who diffused it widely elsewhere. They saw in it new prospects, an opening up of their fields of activity and the possibility of raising their strategies and stakes to the world level. Above all they regarded it as political and moral legitimization of their function. The majority accepted, without criticism, this vision of development and with their usual drive they took on the role of major players in globalization. They continued to think that the common good was in the hands of the public authorities, and therefore their responsibility was restricted to developing their firms in the framework of the buoyant competitive battles of creativity and technical progress. They had little concern for ethical or political questions. They left it to the law to determine the common good and the rules of the game, which was normal practice in advanced countries. They did not question whether the basic principles of such a system could still function in a beneficial way in the absence of rules and economic policies at the global level.

The logic of the market economy is transformed into an ideology when individuals believe they can apply it in a global way and forget concrete realities such as asymmetries of power, unequal development, protectionism by powerful countries, and historical and cultural differences. They embark on a course of instrumental logic when they reject all goals but the efficient functioning of the system itself.

What is at stake here is the globalization of a development model that avoids international political debate and is practised without the rules of the game being properly laid down, without the international institutions being able to secure their acceptance and without taking into consideration the social, cultural and political interests of the weakest countries and social categories.

It is a question of an ideology that attempts to transform a simplified economic logic into a unique model for development and progress. This is based on the conviction that, if left to itself, the market is the instrument of universal progress.

Pushed to its limits, it tries to decouple politics from economics and grant the latter almost complete autonomy. For some it even tends to become a dogma that is improper to contest. 'Free world trade has become a sacrosanct principle of modern economic theory, a universal dogma, a true religion whose premises it is forbidden to challenge.'[3]

As for the firm, this ideology transforms it into a profit-generating machine and thus reduces it to a mere financial entity. Its purpose is to enrich the shareholder and this is the only measure of its performance. It is therefore locked into a logic of means that separates it completely from its social ends and its citizenship dimension. The firm therefore runs the risk of being governed only by the overwhelming concern for gain. From this viewpoint the dominant ideology is incompatible with the concept of the responsible enterprise.

As we shall see later, neither political leaders nor business leaders have alerted citizens to the dangers of development based solely on the market logic. Rather it is civil society that, through its thousands of non-governmental organizations (NGOs) and active militants, has become the main source of awareness of the problems of globalization and the urgent need to do something about them.

By establishing the economy as an end rather than a means, the single thought is the greatest obstacle to the emergence of responsible firms that the movement for social responsibility wishes to introduce. This ideology is unfit for the contemporary era. It is incapable of shedding ethical or political light on the problems posed by sustainable development and the survival of the planet.

The single thought is *simplistic*: it is scarcely sensitive to the political and cultural diversity and complexity of the world (Urban, 2000). When it claims that economic progress has its own logic and that the state has only to look after the remainder, it ignores the accelerating pace of development and the fact that the law can only follow with considerable delay. It also ignores the fact that supervisory and control bodies are often outstripped by and never possess as much information as managers. It ignores the power of the players to influence the direction taken by society and the new responsibilities it imposes on them.

The single thought is *exaggeratedly optimistic*. Its faith in the efficiency of the markets, the virtue of the technosciences and the capacity to adapt structures allows it to ignore competitive inequalities, the ambiguity of technologies and the social and psychological cost of restructuring and disintegration. Like Pangloss it repeats with false naïvety that, as long as one continues on one's way, everything is – or will be – for the best, the best of all possible worlds.

The single thought is *conservative*. It is convinced that its development model is the best and only one. It does not need changing or reforming. This is what the Cato Institute, a defender of this ideology, has to say: 'The market economy as well as the liberty it safeguards and the prosperity it secures are threatened, not as in the recent past by the firebrands who seek to abolish it, but by more modest tinkerers who seek to "improve" it in the name of myriad social concerns.'[4] For the conservatives, any reform can only be destructive or impractical.

The single thought is *intolerant and arrogant.* It does not tolerate being contradicted or questioned. Those who criticize it are systematically classified as utopians, dreamers or pure theorists, or are accused of lying, cheating or wanting to destroy the system. Some go even further: referring to the limits that the EU wanted to place on drug advertising, a director of a large pharmaceutical firm said: 'We are talking about censure here. I would even say that we are faced with dictatorship.'[5]

Another example of the arrogance of the single thought is the comments of a German economist on the European constitution project. The project

> ignores the market economy, it says nothing about the protection of property, it does not involve itself with either the freedom of enterprise or the division of work; instead, it proposes doubtful secondary objectives such as sustainable development or balanced economic growth; harmonization of social protection will lead to the deindustrialization of entire regions; there is no place in the sun for a unique European model, etc. (Sinn, 2003)

When business leaders are locked into a single thought they become like those people in the *Ancien Régime* described by Mirabeau: 'often wrong, but never in doubt'.

The single thought is *more financial than economic* because its main model and central objective are expressed in terms of profit, which puts it nearer to the lure of profit or even cupidity than to economic progress or sustainable development. A recent study of the perception of the firm[6] reveals that the most widely read book in the US after the Bible is *Atlas Shrugged* by Ayn Rand. It is the story of a businessman who invents perpetual motion but is forced to share his profits with his less successful competitors. The question is, what would happen if Atlas – that is, capitalism – grew tired of carrying the world on his shoulders. In an astonishing passage the businessman praises the virtues of money:

If you ask me to name the proudest distinction of Americans, I would choose, because it contains all the others, the fact that they were the people who created the phrase 'to make money'. No other language or nation had ever used these words. Before men have always thought of wealth as a static quantity, to be seized, begged, inherited, shared, looted or obtained as a favour. Americans were the first to understand that wealth has to be created. The words 'to make money' hold the essence of human morality. (Rand, 1996)

The single thought is a way of eliminating politics and ethics from the firm's choices. When the market economy becomes an ideology it severs the dimension of citizenship, thereby ensuring that its actions automatically contribute to the general interest. 'There is nothing more dangerous than an idea when it is only a single idea' (Alain, quoted in de Brabandère, 1998).

In order to be taken seriously, firms that wish to be responsible must have the courage to escape from this simplistic ideology and rethink their purpose and culture. If the firm does not exert its power more explicitly in favour of the common good and subject itself to ethical values, it risks undemocratically imposing on us a form of development that we do not want.

The weakness of the nation-state

While the economic and financial games have become world-wide, the power to regulate the economy, restrict it and suppress excesses has largely remained national, despite the efforts of the EU and certain world institutions. Consider the contrast between the funds available to states to enable them to govern (between 30 per cent and 50 per cent of GNP) and the paucity of resources devoted to world governance.

Economic globalization is developing in a legal environment that is often overregulated at the national level, or at least in Europe and Japan, but underregulated at the world level. This has two adverse effects: it does not allow global problems to be dealt with, and it places firms in extremely unequal positions in international competition. To remain competitive, firms must be able to play by the same rules: uniform environmental and security standards, reciprocity in opening up frontiers and so on. This puts states under constant pressure from firms that do not have a choice: they must obtain from their governments a sufficient relaxation of social, legal and environmental constraints, or they will become weak or be forced to relocate some of their activities. This is doubtless a caricature, but states are subject to constant pressure from firms in the interest of greater competitiveness. Firms sometimes even resort to employment blackmail. And governments try as well as they can to achieve a balance between all the interests at stake.

As we shall see, those who criticize the poor regulation of globalization accuse the state of placing itself at the service of the competitiveness of firms. It does this to support the economy and preserve employment. This is rooted in the more general framework of structural reforms aimed at modernizing the economic system and making it comparable to the most successful one: the archetypal American model.

The EU is moving partly in the same direction, as illustrated by the Lisbon declaration (2000), which announced the ambitious objective of making the EU the world's most competitive economic power. The EU's reports on competitiveness reveal a great understanding of the processes behind it, but only pay slight attention to the problems inherent in the aims, values and choices of a less instrumental development model. Moreover the reports are largely inspired by those produced by the European Round Table.[7] While strong on analysis, they are completely steeped in the instrumental logic of a competitiveness imposed by a system whose aims and terms are beyond discussion. Yet again the premises of reason are not considered.

Nonetheless the proposed EU constitution speaks of sustainable development and a social market economy. Is this compatible with the above-mentioned hypercompetitive process? Long-term sustainability means that we will have to improve our development model at a world level.

When addressing the problems posed by globalization, one must recognize that the states are increasingly helpless. As Raymond Aron (1983) has said, the nation-states are too large for the small problems and too small for the great ones. A question is often half-ironically asked nowadays: 'Who will unite the world if McDonald's don't?'

One only has to consider a few examples of actions by firms to appreciate the unsuitability of the current political structures.[8]

In the case of successive *oil slicks*, it took the *Prestige*[9] catastrophe for control measures to begin to be implemented. What could a country do in the face of the following: a Liberian tanker with a Greek captain and Asian crew, flying the convenience flag of the Bahamas, managed by Greek shipowners and chartered by the Swiss subsidary of a Russian firm?

Like the *Prestige*, oil tankers are often registered in countries that impose few regulations. The crews work in poor conditions, and ships often set sail without complying with basic safety standards (Crivallero, 2002). This is an example of the freight market imposing its will. Maritime trade has never ceased to grow, and the use of old ships helps to keep down costs. Pressure from shipowners and the liberal ideology of governments have until now prevented such ships from being decommissioned. Some regulations have been introduced but the political will to enforce them is seriously lacking. The European Commission has reacted strongly, but many illegal maritime practices are beyond the reach of the EU.

More generally, *pollution of the planet* and other environmental damage continue to increase: greenhouse gas emissions, acid rain, water pollution, the exhaustion of groundwater, the elimination of species and so on.

Neither the US nor the EU alone can deal with these problems effectively, even if they did have the political will to do so. Only a world-wide effort will suffice. The Kyoto Protocol (1997) on climate change was a step in this direction, but we are all aware of the US response to it: in the words of president George W. Bush, the role of the US president is to look after the interests of American industry.[10]

Once again the market, competitive constraints and the imperatives of short-term profitability are prevailing over the global common good, which is poorly defined and lacking a common political will and the means of applying it any exist. For 50 years the countless international conventions initiated in this area by the United Nations have had no decisive impact.

Another example is the *regulation of the internet*. Capable of the best and the worst, the internet is hard to control. If there is a global phenomenon it is the internet, and the nation-states are incapable of regulating it. Would a more global approach be more successful? It is impossible to give a precise answer.

An interesting example of the need for regulation is the protection of personal privacy. Another is respect for intellectual or artistic property. One could also mention the control and suppression of cybercrime. The invasion of unsolicited e-mail messages (spam) is considered by some to be a legal catastrophe and a new ethical problem. It is a question of the private 'occupation' of public property such as the broadband network. This may make cyberspace off-limits for children and unpleasant for adults.

If one thinks of *the media* and the powerful support for education and culture they could provide, again the law of the market (audience ratings) too often holds sway over the longer-term objectives or values of public policies. In the excitement of the AOL-Time Warner merger, one executive declared that media groups had become more important than governments, NGOs and teaching institutions.

Regulation of the financial system is above all needed at the international level.

> Faced with a globalized financial system, an isolated state in fact finds itself powerless to act. Since the dismantling, at the beginning of the 1970s, of the international monetary system put in place in 1944 by the Bretton Woods treaty, there is strictly speaking no longer any coherent financial and monetary regulation at the world level. Some speak discreetly of a non-system. For Robert Triffin, the acronym IMS now no longer means International Monetary System but International Monetary Scandal. In his view, the scandal lies above all in the fact that the states find themselves stripped of one of the essential prerogatives of sovereignty in favour of an elusive and irresponsible market system that has very unwisely been dressed up with all the virtues of wisdom and rationality. To the point where its responsibility is to discipline the monetary and economic policies of states, whose chief merit henceforth is to gain credibility vis-à-vis the market. (Cobbaut, 1997)

At this point we should mention the biggest challenge of the present: *world poverty*. Neither the nation-states nor the globalized market economy are capable of dealing adequately with the absolute poverty endured by more than a billion people. This involves horrific conditions in respect of health, access to drinking water, food, shelter, work and safety. We know that the market economy cannot, by itself, solve this complex problem. In some cases it even makes it worse.

What do governments, the United Nations and the EU do? Very little, mere crumbs compared with the size of the problem.

Development aid has fallen to ridiculously low levels, whereas the mechanisms of competition have continued to develop and, in the poorest countries, destroy the already weak economic foundations. The customs barriers erected by the rich countries to hinder the importation of agricultural products and textiles have put a real brake on the development of poor countries, as well as revealing the hypocrisy of the former and the inanity of their belief in the values of the market. The EU and United Nations are trying as much as they can to level out the game. This demonstrates an unselfish political will, but they are often made powerless by the resistance of certain states or the ambiguity of the solutions proposed: monetary policies, austerity plans and so on.

What is true for poverty also applies to security, crime prevention, world peace, health care, population migration and many other major problems. The majority of these are beyond the reach of the nation-state, the methods of international governance are still unclear and there are no adequate means of intervention.

As far as peace keeping is concerned, the debate on whether there should be unilateral or collective intervention in Iraq was a recent example of this. The same goes for the preventive action that some states (Australia, the US) want to be able to take against terrorist threats. One might also question the progress made with the treaty for the non-proliferation of nuclear weapons.

In matters of health, globalization holds out the promise of complete eradication of diseases that have plagued humanity for centuries. In the rich countries this has already happened with many diseases, but those which lie outside the logic of the markets – that is, the tropical diseases like malaria and beri-beri – have not been tackled with the same determination. The means belatedly adopted for the fight against AIDS are insufficient to stop this scourge. Without a global approach we could be taken by surprise by the appearance of new diseases that spread rapidly as a result of international mobility. The recent case of atypical pneumonia (SARS) could be seen as an early warning of this.

International law and its institutional structures are ill-suited to these new situations. We are facing the challenges of the future in a political vacuum, without global regulation or a world-wide democratic approach.

One of the causes of this is that the most powerful states are imposing their development model, economic power and national interests on the globalization process. In a world that is tending to become unipolar the US, champion of the unregulated economy and home to powerful firms, is forcing the pace of liberalization, deregulation and opening up, while reserving the right not to conform to rules that disturb these firms and their interests.

This brings us back to economic power strategies that are used to the detriment of weaker states and firms.

> Only a complete misunderstanding of economic policy and naïve optimism can fail to recognize that the inevitable trend towards economic expansion...will lead to the time when power alone will determine each country's share in the economic domination of the world and thus the standard of living of its population, in particular that of its working class (Weber, 1964).

To this can be added citizens' lack of confidence in and weakening commitment to the formal political game: that of democratic parties and institutions at the local and national levels. In a society oriented towards material progress, individualism reigns and is organized more around the computer and television than collective activities and political ties. This reduces the participation of citizens in their institutions and their interest in those who lead them.

Political movements have given way to pressure groups, such as industrial lobbyists and NGOs (Skocpol, 2003). This is what the economist Fitoussi (2003) calls 'the peaceful regression of democracy', and it partly explains why the questioning of our development model takes place in Davos or Porto Alegre rather than in our political and governmental institutions.

Political awakening

The continued absence of so many political figures from this debate is disturbing. They seem to think that the levers for change are not available, and even that globalization driven solely by the market does not constitute a problem.

It is essential for them to return to the stage and to organize a political debate between the main players in this development, not just firms and unions but also NGOs, universities and institutions concerned with ethics. This democratic preparation for a desirable future should occur not only at the national level but also at the European and world levels.

To date the most convincing steps have been taken at the supranational level by the UN and EU. The extraordinary uniting of Europe over the past 50 years shows the possibility of political adaptation when there is a common project and true leaders. In the area that concerns us, the EU has become a force for change.

At the initiative of the European Commission, for example, a forum was set up to outline the conditions for sustainable development. This only represents a start, but industry has shown itself to be open to the approach. The framework for a European strategy for sustainable development was decided at Gothenburg in 2002. The proposed constitution states that 'the Union will work to create a Europe of sustainable development based on balanced growth and a social market economy . . . with a high degree of protection and improvement of the environment' (Article 3). The Commission also supports the 1997 Kyoto Protocol, promotes the introduction of measures to prevent oil spillage, supervises respect for human rights in international economic life, and so on.

But the EU's capacity for action is restricted. It often encounters resistance by member states and sectoral lobbies. Furthermore it is still strongly influenced by and has excessive confidence in the values of the market. We recall the famous passage in the Bangemann report (1994) on the information and communication society: 'It seems to us that Europe must trust and entrust to the private sector the care of transforming Europe into an information society.' This report has guided the Commission's policies in a field in which the stakes are not only information but also culture and education. If one reflects on the influence that technology and private investment will have in this sector, one can understand why citizens are concerned that the direction and pace of this change might be left, without debate, to private initiative alone.

The Commission's policy on competition is another area in which political will is beginning to be felt. Some of its decisions have been strongly criticized for their methodology or lack of rigour, and it could be asked whether its competition policy is sufficiently linked to sustainable development or other EU social or cultural policies.

One positive development is the rise of a militant civil society and NGOs. These are multiplying and becoming a notable oppositional force.[11] They are often highly international and are beginning to have a real influence on the minds of citizens and the behaviour of economic players. As we shall see, the most enlightened firms are willing to listen to the most serious-minded NGOs and to explain their actions in controversial areas.

But many businesses see NGOs as enemies: they reject dialogue and would like to block the globalization process if not destroy it. One can understand this, for many NGOs want to sign up to a relationship of force and are organizing themselves into a world-wide opposition to neoliberal globalization. They intend to 'stimulate local struggles and create a world-wide spread of resistance' (Houtart and Samir, 2002). There is a vast amorphous grouping (Jacquet, 2001), some elements of which are characterized by excess, contradiction and demagogic simplification. But one should not underestimate the importance of their role or the capacity for action by the antiglobalization movement they have launched. This movement has contributed to the failure on world-wide negotiations on foreign direct investment, mobilized public opinion through intelligent use of the media and the internet, influenced authorities and begun to participate in the new consultations on the future of society.[12]

If we accept that our economic model must move in the direction of sustainable development, the most serious-minded NGOs are there to remind us of the necessity and urgency of this. They doubtless do more in this respect than governments and the majority of business leaders.

If we want to fill the political vacuum that characterizes globalization today, it is necessary for economic players to engage in dialogue and cooperation with these new representatives of civil society. These people will not accept unequal dialogue and will only cooperate as equal partners. They liken themselves to the workers' movements of the nineteenth century, which were only able to make their voices heard by joining forces.

Should we recall that after world-war two a true dialogue was established between business and labour and that it was the start of a significant social and even economic progress? The stridence of dispute with NGOs must not prevent firms from participating in these new forms of consultation.

What do not yet exist are new forms of governance that would allow global common good to be expressed and networks, structures and rules established for their implementation, especially in the field of economics. The UN wishes to be a force for change. It has stepped up its appeals, warnings and proposals, but it has relatively little influence and its approaches are scattered, if not contradictory.

In recent years the International Monetary Fund (IMF) has become an active agent of a purist and severe monetarism, a reflection of the 'single thought', which doubtless has had as many negative as positive effects (Stiglitz, 2002). In the meantime the World Bank has not been very successful in reducing inequality in or sufficiently developing the countries with which it has been involved. However it must be credited with introducing a large number of small projects that have really improved the life of the people who have benefited from them. We shall return later to the role of the IMF and World Bank.

The World Trade Organization has helped to open up frontiers. Its objectives are to accelerate and regulate globalization, but without sufficient links with other institutions, such as the International Labour Organization, it risks becoming locked into a vision of globalization that reflects the dominant ideology rather than promotes sustainable development.

The UN secretary general, Kofi Annan, encourages firms to engage in partnerships and cooperative ventures that subscribe to sustainable development (the Global Compact). He is convinced that firms can play a major role and that better use should be made of their capacities on a world scale. This is another sign of political awakening. But are all these initiatives enough to make the system evolve? We shall return to this in the final chapter.

A code of ethics overtaken

Scientific progress and economic globalization are creating problems that traditional ethics are not equipped to handle. Totally new questions have arisen and our moral judgement criteria are not able to inform us on the directions to take. In this regard we can mention genetic engineering, global warming and the inequalities and injustices of the development model.

The philosopher Hans Jonas (2000) reminds us that traditional ethics deal with proximity and simultaneity: 'love your neighbour as yourself', 'do unto others as you would have them do unto you', or 'ethics begins with the first cry of human suffering' (Fourez, 1988). The subjects of these ethics are those near to us and the immediate and visible consequences of our actions.

But just who is our neighbour? Is it the person we pass every day, or the South African who dies from AIDS?

Is it the injured person at the side of the road, or all those evoked by the murmur of an emergent world-wide conscience?

Is it the child of two or three generations hence, when genetic engineering may have made it a hybrid that is deprived of part of its humanity?

How can we hear the cries of suffering that our ear does not detect?

How can we foresee the consequences of genetic engineering, of rapid economic globalization in a poorly regulated world, of growth that degrades the planet, of the use men will make of such funda-mental scientific discoveries as the mechanisms of life, mastery of the atom, artificial intelligence and so on?

As for the simultaneity between actions and their consequences, this no longer exists for a number of the decisions we have to take. In other words, good intentions do not legitimize actions for whose results we do not hold ourselves responsible.

In the past,

well-being and malaise with which acting had to concern itself were close to action, either in the praxis itself, or in its immediate range and they were not the subject of long-term planning. This proximity of ends was valid for time as well as for space. The effective range of the action was small, the lapse of time for the prediction and determination of the ends and for the imputability was short, and the control of circumstances was restricted. Just conduct had its immediate criteria and its achievement was almost immediate. The long course of consequences was abandoned to chance, to destiny or to providence. In the same way, ethics had to do with the here and now, with the opportunities as they occur between people, with the repetitive and typical situations of private and public life. The good man was the one who responded to these opportunities with virtue and wisdom, who cultivated the faculty within himself and who resigned himself to the unknown. (Jonas, 2000)

The preceding chapters attempted to show that the actions of firms have moved well beyond these traditional boundaries. Mankind is endowed with the technological, economic and financial capacity for actions that cover the world and whose consequences are increasingly distant and difficult to foresee. In essence there is a 'gulf between our technological power and our projected knowledge' (ibid.)

Jonas suggests the need for another major divergence from the old ethics, which related exclusively to the relationship between human beings and was anthropocentric. Today our actions threaten biological diversity, the conditions of life on this planet and even its survival. The stakes are sufficient to broaden the ethical question beyond the relationship between human beings.

These thoughts lead us to believe that in addition to the political deficit there is an ethical vacuum. The rocket of globalization has been launched into this vacuum, guided only by an instrumental logic that deprives it of ethical and political values (Delcourt and de Woot, 2000).

Since firms are the major players in this, the ethical problems bound up with development should concern them first and foremost. Without the adoption of new ethics and broadened aims for economic action, we risk seeing *Homo faber* (able to make tools) gaining the upper hand over *Homo sapiens* and being subject to the growing dominance of means over ends.

Today the true ethical problem is to answer the following question: what sort of society do we want to construct together with the extraordinary means that are available to us? Current business ethics, as practised or taught, are not suited to the contemporary situation. Many executives and managers, locked in an unmerciful competitive struggle, reduce ethics to honesty and respect for the rules. They are not inclined to question the aims of economic and technical progress. For them Prometheus is a hero and his bondage an injustice.

One can understand their attitude when one considers the competitive pressures they endure in an unequal arena. Quite rightly they do not see themselves as being in a position to change the rules. But here as in politics, they try to transfer responsibility for the future to the authorities, to laws that do not yet exist and to a completely outmoded system of ethics. They refuse to consider their actions in terms of power and the long-term effects on the future of society. They lock themselves into the logic of competition, 'stripped of every dignity of purpose' (Jonas, 2000). At the extreme, they behave as though the welfare of the firm is the supreme law (*salus firmae, suprema lex*).

One has only to think of the American attitude towards technological progress and innovative opportunities. They pursue them with eyes closed, convinced it will be cheaper to repair any damage than to suspend or stop 'progress', which is the decisive competitive weapon. And yet, 'for honest men, does everything that can be done have to be done?' (Cicero, 1962).

Another example is collaboration with discredited regimes, sometimes in contravention of international sanctions. One has only to consider the indictment of banks, arms manufacturers and mining firms.

So many decision-makers, locked into this logic, maintain a degree of personal integrity and a morality of proximity and simultaneity that do not reflect the scale of the problems.

As we shall see, the most enlightened leaders take the ethical argument further. This is true of proactive movements such as Corporate Social Responsibility Europe. These leaders ask what should be done to ensure that the firm retains its legitimacy as an agent of economic progress. 'Which wagon must be added to the train of the market economy for it to continue to run?' The answer is not yet clear but the question has at least been posed.

But here again the new ethical dimensions have not really been tackled. They do not question the premises of the system they operate: globalized growth is a benefit and competitiveness is the means of survival. They have not yet asked the true ethical question of our time: what world do we want to build together? Will it really be sufficient to add one more 'wagon' to an incomplete system in order to transform it?

Business schools do little to raise their ethical teaching by including responsibility for the future. These high places of market ideology, these temples of capitalism, rarely teach more than a utilitarian morality. For most of them business ethics merely amount to integrity (certainly the minimum!) Many add that ethics pay.

A large American management school launched a new 'product': leadership in integrity, and business leaders marvelled at it. Other management schools have added a few methodological 'gadgets', such as ethical codes, the benchmarking of good practices and analysis of the most striking cases of dishonesty or of recent scandals.

It is interesting to note that many executives who were the source of these malpractices graduated from the best business schools and applied these superficial and often cosmetic tools to the letter, and not to the spirit. Enron was top of its class for its ethical code. A professor at a large European school of management admitted recently that he did not know how to integrate the ethical dimension into social responsibilities of the firm since economics possessed its own logic!

When a teacher, somewhat more informed on this point than his colleagues, begins to ask the true ethical and political questions about the aims of the system itself, he is generally considered to be like a duck in the brood, without much influence on the evolution of the school, but a useful flag-waver to confront all the external troublemakers who dare to challenge the system.

It is thus not surprising that ethics, in the sense of a world-wide society to be constructed, generates few responses. As much in matters of politics as in matters of morality, the behaviour of power tends to hold sway, confirming the pessimistic view of Max Weber.

One can therefore suggest that the action of the firm operates today with every new weapon of science and technology, in an open, but poorly regulated space, and in a kind of ethical and political vacuum. If it locks itself into a single thought, the firm then risks supporting a system whose dynamism, creativity and coherence work in the manner of a road roller, without any other logic than its own effectiveness and without any other aim than profit for the shareholder.

Montesquieu had already sensed this type of drift when he wrote: 'For the Greeks and the Romans, admiration for political and moral knowledge was carried to a kind of cult. Today, we only have respect for the physical sciences, we are exclusively occupied by them, and political good and evil are, for us, a sentiment rather than an object of knowledge.'

5
An Unsustainable System?

Why do the heathen rage, and the people imagine a vain thing?

(Psalm 2)

Introduction

This book is about the *raison d'être* of the firm in a poorly regulated global economy. There is therefore no question of analyzing here all the problems of the planet, still less of blaming the firm for all the misfortunes of the world. There is never a simple cause of complex problems.

By restricting ourselves to the market economy, in which the firm is the principal player, we can pose the question of whether the current development model, despite its extraordinary creativity, is still acceptable or requires some profound change.

This chapter critically reflects on the dominant economic system, whose deviations have become more apparent. If we are to preserve its qualities of creativity and effectiveness it is necessary to identify its weaknesses, not only in order to denounce them but also to help correct them.

What is at issue is not so much the firm itself as the system it supports. Many business leaders refuse to question this. They strive to make their firm successful and to win the competitive game. They fail to see that the latter has locked them into an instrumental logic whose combined effects may be harmful.

They often take criticisms as personal attacks and find them unjust, given the effort they have made to contribute to economic prosperity, employment and the raising of living standards. They find it hard to take a step back and consider the development model into which their firm fits. 'Happy are the princes who suffer a bitter piece of advice' (Mirabeau quoted in Michelet, 1974).

Many managers still cling to their fundamental belief in the virtues of the model; it is good because it is effective. The most dedicated believers are the business schools that train the majority of managers and future heads of firms. However, neither the Coué method (repetition to convince oneself and others) nor the ostrich policy is worthy of responsible executives. Continuing to repeat that the current system is the only valid one, without acknowledging its dangers, will hardly serve the cause they defend. Accusing critics of mental retardation, attachment to the past and harking back to the nineteenth century merely conceals an absence of reflection and a refusal to question anything.

Some change in their thinking is however beginning to appear,[1] but as we have already seen it is often restricted to asking 'which wagon must be added to the train for it to continue to run', without realizing that the train is moving faster and faster but without adequate goals or values.

The real question is whether one is responsible for the perverse effects of the system in which one operates and which one supports. Can one act justly in a system that is not just? Must one restrict oneself to changing a few details or should one strive to correct its defects and change its direction? These are the kinds of question that the responsible firm must ask itself.

We therefore need to consider whether, in the current ethical and political vacuum, the dynamic of economic globalization is leading us towards a model that will be politically unsustainable and morally unacceptable. It is necessary to understand the mechanisms that could cause the model to go off course. In this chapter we shall examine three types of drift that oblige us to transform the model radically: systemic drift, financial drift and behavioural drift.

Abuse, cheating and scandal will also be discussed but they will not be central to the investigation, firstly because they are far from widespread, and secondly because they are more easily corrected.

Systemic drift and deviation

Acceleration

The pace of economic and technical change is accelerating as a result of global competition. We have embarked on a race whose speed is dictated by the dynamism of firms and the competitive game.

The pace is often faster than that of change in political, civic and institutional society. This time lag increases the danger of inequality, exclusion, unemployment and social breakdown: the system begins to crush people (see Crozier and Friedberg, 1977; Touraine, 1992). By increasing pollution, the acceleration of growth also endangers the future of the planet. As for the advancement of science, this presents us with more problems than we are able to solve.

If the logic of economic and technical innovation is one of creative destruction, we might well ask whether the destructive effects are beginning to outweigh the beneficial effects of creativity. In other words, is not the cost of rapid change becoming too high? Let us look at some examples.

The race for technical progress has become so fast that many contestants are obliged to drop out. Society is increasingly being divided into those who are capable of running because they have the necessary skills to use the instruments of progress, and those who are left behind. The latter is obviously true of developing countries.

It is also true of unqualified workers. Are we going to allow them to sink into long-term unemployment or restrict themselves to small jobs, or must we reduce their unemployment benefit in order to make them seek work? Their plight illustrates the worrying backwardness of our policies on education and lifetime training.

The same goes for older workers. When a large international firm declares that engineers over 50 are no longer able to adapt to developments in their sector we are faced with a worrying social drift.

It is also true of managers, from whom utmost adaptability is expected. Witness the surprise of a director of training when he heard a senior member of a large management school address new graduates in these terms: 'in a difficult and hard world, may you have great will and great strength; in a complex world, may you become capable of being multifunctional and multi-skilled; in a changing world, prepare yourselves to change firms or occupations frequently and to challenge yourself almost permanently.'[2]

Is this really the world we want? Does not such a system crush the player? Is it not the replacement of 'being' by 'doing'? What are the aims and purpose of this frenzied race? Where do we find Paul Valéry's (1988) 'leisure to mature and purpose to last'?

The acceleration of industrialization, trade and competition is also beginning to attack the planet. Pollution reduction has become a major priority: rising temperatures, the deterioration of the ozone layer, the growing shortage of water and the reduction of biodiversity are global problems generated by an unbridled growth model.

Much of global warming is due to man's actions. The consequences are starting to emerge: droughts in some areas, flooding in others, rising sea levels and so on. Pollution and climate change are a direct result of the difference in pace between economic action and public counteraction. 'We emit more and more greenhouse gas while stripping the forests that normally absorb it' (Retallack, 2001a).

Economic globalization is accelerating this formidable phenomenon by intensifying industrial activity, promoting overconsumption, spreading a poorly regulated development model and driving the privatization of almost every activity. Pollution is directly linked to this economic activity. With only 4.6 per cent of the world's population the US accounts for 25 per cent of greenhouse gas emissions. Imagine what will become of the planet when China and India are industrialized and choked with vehicles.

The acceleration in trade is having the same effect. Between 1959 and 1997 world trade grew 15-fold and the current means of transportation use fossil fuels that add considerably to pollution (Retallack, 2001b).

To cater to the rapid development of the economy the world's resources are being depleted through overmining, overfishing, deforestation and so on. Global fish stocks, for example, are being decimated by factory trawlers using nets that are 30 kilometres long ('walls of death').

As for fresh water, overconsumption by agricultural and industrial producers has completely altered the water cycle. Producing one kilo of beef in can take 20 thousand litres of water, a ton of steel 280 thousand litres, and a kilo of paper 700 litres (Martou, 2003).

Such excessive use of water is threatening the entire ecosystem, all parts of which are dependent on the availability of water (Roche,

2000). The International Institute for Water Management predicts that consumption will increase by 50 per cent over the next 20 years, so if we do not change our policies and priorities there will no longer be sufficient water to supply our households and agriculture. Moreover water, unlike oil, has no substitute.

The impact of agricultural, forestry and fishing practices on biodiversity is of a similar if not greater magnitude than that of the great prehistoric extinctions (Dron, 2000):

> From the tertiary to the present day, the maximum rate of disappearance has been one species every 50 to 100 years...Estimates are that 50 000 species of plant will disappear between now and 2050. If one takes an average of 20 species of insect and other arthropods that are dependent on these plants, that represents a minimum of a million species. (Ramade, 1993)

It is important to reiterate here the link between the current development model and the deterioration of the planet, not to mention the danger to the health of mankind. Do we need to mention other excesses resulting from the race for 'progress' and the desire for growth at any cost? Feeding cattle with products that contain meat, thus causing 'mad cow disease', is symptomatic of a blinkered attitude that could only be the product of the single thought.[3]

Some chemical additives intended to enhance the taste of food products, make them more attractive or prolong their shelf life damage the health of those who consume them. The American will to impose transgenic crops is rooted in the same furious race to conquer world markets.

The acceleration of scientific and technical progress is also starting to exceed our capacity for ethical and political adaptation. This type of progress often occurs, without debate, through force of circumstance and the dynamism of firms.

We have seen how advances in biotechnology are outpacing our ethical thinking. The case of Jamie Whitaker, the first 'saviour' test-tube baby shows that dangerous frontiers have already been crossed (Prowse, 2003). The embryo that became Jamie was selected over several others because it offered the possibility of curing Jamie's brother of a chronic illness. The baby was therefore a means of fulfilling a purpose that was not its own. 'Human nature is thus beginning to be inexorably instrumentalized. Embryos are increasingly treated as any kind of laboratory raw material... Biotechnology firms hope to create a genetic supermarket where parents will be able to shop for the desirable qualities for their future children' (Prowse, 2003).

With regard to genetically modified organisms (GMOs), the American attitude towards these is less prudent (more dynamic?) than that of Europe. It amounts to pressing ahead as quickly as possible and correcting any damage later. This attitude is clearly strengthened by the ideology of the market and competition. One result is that some countries have been politically powerless to resist the invasion of this type of 'progress' before the completion of adequate studies of the consequences. This applies in particular to Mexico, which has been obliged to adopt transgenic maize in order not to lose this type of agricultural product from its economy.

In the world of the internet, new methods of competition and piracy have appeared. For example it is now possible to swap or download music for free, to the detriment of the recording industry, which has recently suffered a 31 per cent fall in sales. The regulation of competition has not been able to keep up with this development. The same applies to the prevention of IT crime.

Another example of failing to adapt can be found in the financial sector. Inventiveness there has reached the point where it has become difficult, if not impossible, to understand the set-ups built on derivative products or to evaluate their systemic risks. The financier Warren Buffet recently described them as a delayed action bomb in the capitalist system, or even a potential weapon of mass destruction. Hans Eichel, the German finance minister, also thinks that they constitute a real threat to global financial stability (*Financial Times*, 7 February 2002). Here again the development model is racing away and seems to be evading all control. It is not surprising that anti-establishment voices speak of a runaway train, a fast car about to hit a wall, a disaster of *Titanic* proportions, and so on.

It is certain that the accelerated use of this poorly regulated and poorly targeted model is disturbing those whom it marginalizes, and those who think that economic development should only be a means and not an end in itself.

At the global level, one can understand why it has discouraged those who feel incapable of catching up, causing them to lock themselves into other forms of single thought, such as political or religious fundamentalism.

Market orientation

Economic and technical progress is being directed more and more exclusively by firms and the 'invisible hand' of the market. The following are a few examples.

Firms accumulate a growing volume of knowledge resources thanks to their enormous efforts in research and development. They are the ones that decide on the *type of research* they will do, and because of this the nature of the new products or services they will offer to consumers.

Of course this is based on market indications, which one might think is the best way to direct resources. But this is only partly true: the invisible hand only serves the creditworthy as its criteria are exclusively commercial and financial. Consider pharmaceutical firms: because the financial returns would be low they do not give priority to research on drugs designed to treat illnesses in poor countries (orphan drugs); rather they invest considerable amounts of money in studying the problems of obesity and impotence in rich countries. Of the 1393 new drugs approved between 1975 and 1999 only 16, or just over 1 per cent, were developed specifically for tropical illnesses and tuberculosis, which represent some 11.4 per cent of the global incidence of illness (*Financial Times*, 23 May 2003).

The same goes for technical progress. Consider the digital revolution. To date the information society has developed almost exclusively in response to the needs of the market and audience ratings. For example the major innovation, television, far from catering to educational needs has plunged people into a culture of consumption, zapping between channels and entertainment.

It is true that the internet allows people more choice. They are able to surf the net by using criteria other than those of the commercial channels. Once again this shows how technical progress is neutral and can be put to the best or the worst use. We shall return to this in the following section.

More important still is the *geographic orientation of development.* It too depends on the market game.

When profitability dominates the force of the market economy is naturally directed at profitable regions. This is how the process of competitiveness, already described, has developed in the advanced countries. Over the years it concentrated on the triad of North America, Western Europe and Japan, then gradually expanded to certain regions of South-East Asia. The recent adoption of this process by the highly regulated China, whose market is huge, perhaps signals the emergence of a special development model – open but closely supervised and strongly directed.

Those countries which have not succeeded in mastering the challenges of the market economy are kept on the periphery. Multinational firms often only invest in them in order to benefit from their natural resources or lower costs. Perhaps in the long term such investments will assist the economic rise of Latin America, Africa and the Middle East, but at the moment this is not the case.

Inequality has grown and poverty remains widespread. Although they can increase wealth, the market and the invisible hand are incapable of ensuring equitable distribution. The mechanisms of redistribution put in place by states do not exist at the global level and inequality continues to grow.

The gap between rich and poor countries stood at 3 to 1 in 1820; it rose to 10 to 1 in 1900, 30 to 1 in 1960, 60 to 1 in 1990 and 74 to 1 in 1999. Of the world's six billion inhabitants, 1.3 billion live below the poverty line, which is less than $1 per day (World Bank, 1999). Health expenditure is $2800 per inhabitant in the OECD countries; in Africa it is $20. Even in the rich countries there is the spectre of unemployment and exclusion. Some claim that a more liberal economy could remedy this. Others, including myself, think that it is the sad result of the purely commercial orientation of development and a pace of change that is too rapid for societies to be able to adapt to without causing suffering. One of today's major challenges is to reconcile the dynamism of the market economy with social justice.

Another question is whether there is a link between globalization and the increase in inequality. A World Bank study has shown that opening up to world trade is negatively correlated with growth in the income of the 40 per cent poorest of the population and positively correlated with income growth in for the other 60 per cent (Lundberg and Squire, 1999; see also Lundberg and Milanovic, 2000). The costs of adjusting to international opening up are completely borne by the poorest, whatever the duration of this adjustment. It therefore seems that liberal globalization has 'punished the poorest in the world and the workers while favouring the richest and the ruling elites' (Hertsgaard, 2002).

Inequality relates not only to income but also to the knowledge and skills of economic and technical modernity. The division between those who have the necessary skills and tools (the 'haves') and those who do not (the 'have-nots') exists in every area of life and work: education, the ability to adapt, access to information and the means of manipulating it, preventive medicine, the quality of organizations and their management, scientific capacity and so on. The acceleration of economic and technical change risks increasing these inequalities, or at least in the poorest countries. To this we must add the migration of qualified workers to rich countries, the pace of which often outstrips that of internal development of the poor countries.

Nonetheless a slow but steady improvement in some social indicators (health care, reduced infant mortality, better education) suggests that progress is possible if the international political will is there and sufficient resources are made available.[4]

The major challenge of globalization is to implement, at the world level, the necessary policies and means for sustainable development. The market economy and current ideology have not achieved this, even though for the first time in the history of mankind there are sufficient technical, organizational and financial capabilities to help the whole of humanity to emerge from simple subsistence. Room for manoeuvre now exists, as does an extraordinary capacity for action by successful firms. What is lacking is the political will to transform the development model.

Invasion of the non-commercial world

Here we are speaking of the introduction into the market of goods that arise from a common inheritance or from sectors that have collective stakes: health, humanitarianism, peace, culture, education, security and so on.

The growing invasion of these private and not completely marketable areas poses a key question: what type of society do we wish to create? Is it what will emerge from a democratic debate on the common good, or is it what the law of the market, competition and the powerful advertising machines required by modern marketing will impose on us? This question applies in many areas. We shall look at some cases in the cultural and scientific sectors, where the line between private action and public service is particularly blurred.

In the cultural domain, the power of the giant multimedia groups has reached the point where they are able to dominate and threaten cultural diversity.

The influence of groups such as Time-Warner, Walt Disney and News Corporation continues to grow. We have already seen the power that they rightly or wrongly attribute to themselves: they believe themselves to be more influential than governments, educational institutions and NGOs. They are progressively steering the domains of leisure and entertainment towards what they understand by education ('edutainment'). If we allow the American media groups to dominate the scene our children will be introduced to *The Iliad* and *The Odyssey* by Mickey Mouse and Donald Duck. Is that what we want? It might be thought that the internet will prevent this development, but we should not underestimate the power of these groups to occupy and influence all such networks.

The situation is the same for films, where despite the internet there is a real danger of a reduction in diversity. The economic weight of some countries allows them to impose their cultural products on the whole of the world. Take the example of the American movie industry.[5] There are several good reasons why it dominates the world market. The first is economic: films are easily exported and this advantage is cumulative. The second reason is the quality of these films: the American movie industry is one of the best in the world and has developed exceptional know-how. The third reason is cultural: the American melting pot has created a unique mass culture but the common denominator is sufficiently high for many people in the world to recognize themselves in an American film. These three factors are obviously positive, but in combination they could lead to a reduction in global cultural diversity. This very real danger must be addressed by encouraging and supporting film making in the majority of countries that do not have the means to resist the financial power of American producers. Of course this will be rejected by those who see culture as a merchandise like any other.

One can mention another source of cultural drift: advertising. The majority of the TV channels, especially private ones, have become the means of transforming of merchandise into culture, since advertising revenues have a decisive influence on the programmers' choices.

In a society directed by the market, advertising plays a huge role. In many cases 'TV making is creating, between each screenful of advertising, a sufficiently attractive content for the advertising to have an audience' (*Le Figaro*, August 2002). Audience ratings tend to become the dominant and the most reductive criterion for media policy, killing any attempt to develop a cultural orientation worthy of the name. Italian TV provides a good illustration of this.

Advertising pervades everything and occupies a large place in the collective imagination. All is sacrificed to the market imperative. In order to sell, advertisers sometimes employ highly dubious and questionable methods. So much for advertising codes of ethics. Some agencies respect nothing. In the name of freedom of expression, and often showing no respect, they use and manipulate the values, circumstances and vulnerability of the young. Some bank advertisements have recently driven children to demand more money from their parents – and to draw up a contract for this, because one never knows when Alzheimer's disease might strike.

One advertising poster by a car manufacturer uses a photograph that resembles an internet picture designed to attract paedophile tourists to Thailand: the front view of three young girls and the back view of a young man – the caption suggestively invites the reader to 'Come and try the new little ones'. Can we be surprised by the disgust of some people and their questioning of an economic system without values?

> Would that these new masters of thought, these monsters of communication, these guarantors of the world's advancement and morality take a look at what is inside their heads, and that the sick people who have imagined and invented this advertising crap in their hearts and brains might pay damages with interest to the parents of the victims' (Ide, 2003).

Let us now turn to the press. Its freedom is a central element of democracy and everyone knows the influence it can exert in the political and cultural domains. It is precisely this that confers on it social responsibilities and should prevent it from seeing itself as an exclusively marketing activity. The vision of its role and its hierarchy of values are therefore of considerable importance.

The traditional purpose of the quality press is to serve society by informing it objectively, opening up debate and offering perspectives. In a way it is like a public service. Quality is essential and the art of managing a large newspaper is finding a balance between quality and profitability. When the criterion of maximum profit prevails, the sense responsibility weakens and quality tends to fall.

An interesting example is the American press group that, in the 1980s, Dean Singleton built up in the space of less than eight years by buying 71 newspapers. This venture was based on a purely financial footing and a brutal strategy of cost reduction that went through the following stages: buy the paper, cut the staffing level, lower the quality, reduce objectivity and raise the advertising rates (Coleridge, 1993).

Similarly Ralph Ingersoll, who brought together 240 newspapers in less than five years with the only view to tripling their profitability, declared: 'my idea of a *good* newspaper is the difference between a yield of 10% and a yield of 30%' a purely financial way of seeing a newspaper.

When profit maximization becomes the dominant criterion, the orientation of a newspaper is increasingly dependent on advertising and its quality can only deteriorate. This is the same drift that takes place in other media when they allow themselves to be ruled by audience ratings.

Competition also lowers the tone of newspaper coverage about people. 'Restraint is thrown overboard. The dividing line between legitimate news and "soft" news is completely blurred . . . [in the face of competition] old columnists are replaced by a team of aggressive voyeurs who no longer subscribe to the rules of the profession which begins to become disgraceful' (Kelleher, 2003).

In the domain of scientific knowledge, firms are increasingly appropriating new discoveries, patenting them and transforming them into new products. They then turn them into competitive weapons and direct them according to commercial or financial criteria, without always taking into account the risks that may be involved. A large part of the new scientific heritage thus becomes subject to a marketing logic that controls its use and applications.

A disturbing example in this regard is the race between the private project Celera and the public project to map the human genome.

The fact that some human genome sequences might be patented and cease to be collective property poses a real moral and political question. One should add that the Patent Office in the UK agreed to patent not only the process of animal cloning, as exemplified by Dolly the sheep, but also human embryos cloned by this method. This meant that a human foetus in gestation might become the property of an individual or a firm. This decision by the patent office, taken without political or ethical debate, was subsequently revoked.

A similar situation exists with the excessive protection given to intellectual property, which is preventing the poorest countries from benefiting from advances in medicine. The current efforts by some firms to appropriate and patent the ancestral medical knowledge of the inhabitants of tropical rainforests is but one example of unjust market-oriented practices, even if the intention is to spread knowledge throughout the world.

Let us not forget *the world of sport*, which is becoming a leisure merchandise *par excellence*. The sums of money involved[6] and the advertising strategies linked to it make the Roman games seem like simple village pastimes.

And what of the numerous places where public space has been vandalized by *real estate speculators*, who for years have imposed their purely commercial logic?

More generally, the invasion of non-commercial domains by the private sector poses the question of what constitutes the common heritage and public service. When asserting that the development of the market or international trade are not ends in themselves and that only a proportion of assets come within the market, Pierre Calame proposes an interesting classification:

> The first category consists of the goods and services that are the fruit of our ingenuity and are divided by being shared out, that is, mainly industrial goods and services to people. The market is well adapted to this first category.
>
> The second category consists of assets that are destroyed when shared out; they consist of the huge number of common assets that require collective management: control of the sea and the coastal zones, the tropical forest, the vast steppes, which are still untouched.

The third category consists of assets that are divided by being shared out but do not necessarily imply human activity; they are the natural resources whose distribution arises from social justice rather than the market economy.

The fourth category, which is the most interesting for the future, consists of assets that multiply through being shared out: knowledge, intelligence, beauty, love, experience, etc.; they should not arise from the market but rather from a logic of mutualism: I receive because I give.

By making the market an absolute value... the four categories of assets are reduced to one single category: merchandise. By doing this the second category, consisting of common assets, is destroyed; an act of injustice is committed by restricting the third category, natural resources, to the rich minority... those who do not possess the means to pay their holders are deprived of knowledge and experience. Furthermore one ends up with an economy that ignores the value of relationships. (Calame, 2001)

Is it necessary to privatize transport, health care, education, pensions and even prisons? Is there not a risk of once again exacerbating inequality and neglecting infrastructure? Must we entrust security and peacekeeping to private enterprises?

In the case of water[7] the figures speak for themselves: 1.4 billion people do not have access to drinking water and the dwellings of 3 billion people are not connected to a sewerage system. The consequences are disastrous: 3.4 million human beings, half of whom are children, die every year from illnesses associated with contaminated water. Riccardo Petrella (1998) has led a vigorous compaign for recognition of this problem.

François Martou (2003) wonders whether, in the name of efficiency, the management of water should be left to a few private players. But this risks the disappearance of a public service in favour of a commercial service, including for the 1.4 billion people who do not yet have access to clean water.

The privatization of water supplies was followed by price increases for private consumers and cuts that hit the poorest in society. Opponents of liberal globalization question the abandonment of this resource to the 'invisible hand' and the laws of the market when climate change and pollution are threatening the availability of fresh water. They fear that 'the swimming pools of the rich may take precedence over the drinking water of the poor' (Vandana Shiva, quoted in Martou, 2003). The problem is sufficiently complex not to be restricted to a debate on principles but to explore the possibility of a new approach based on cooperation between the private and public sectors.

In poor countries the public authorities rarely possess the professional and financial resources needed to build the necessary infrastructure and manage it in a satisfactory way. Here the private sector could intervene and provide technical and managerial skills, but in partnership rather than as the dominating force. Some firms regard this type of cooperation as a new way of exercising their social responsibility (see for example Suez-Ondéo, 2000).

Domination and destruction

The situations of dominance and power are generally underestimated and it is too often forgotten that 'between the strong and the weak, between rich and poor, it is freedom that oppresses and the law that frees' (Lacordaire 1996). We have seen that the technosciences and globalization have obliged the firm to develop a strong strategic capacity, and that the mastery of financial, technological, organizational and managerial resources gives it real power.

When this power is exercised in a more or less equal competitive game it can contribute to growth and development, as in the most advanced countries. Competition prevents sustained domination. Monopolies created by innovation are short-lived, technical progress rapidly calls into question the competitive advantage of the first mover. The laws of competition more or less succeed in maintaining equality of opportunity between the players and openings for newcomers.[8]

On the other hand the game is completely unequal in developing countries. Our competition model is imposed on them, a model for which they are ill-prepared and which locks them into a position of weakness. International organizations such as the IMF, the World Bank and the WTO oblige them to open up their frontiers, not to implement any industrial policy worthy of the name, and to practice a budgetary rigour and financial orthodoxy that stem from hardline monetarism. To this is added the conditions they impose in respect of international investment and the protection of intellectual property rights.

Some critics claim that the WTO rules were written with the intention of making illegal the further use of any industrial and technological policy that had proved successful for the capitalist governments of East and South-East Asia when developing their local industries (Wade, 2003). They are thus condemned to remain as producers of raw materials and their terms of trade continue to deteriorate.

It is within this unequal framework that firms deploy their strategies of globalization and investment. It is not surprising that situations of domination or even destruction occur. For example in the context of trade we demand that they dismantle their customs barriers, but we see to it that sections of our economies and markets are protected.

The EU and US agricultural policies are a sad example of domination and unequal trade (Watkins, 2003): every year the rich countries spend more than a billion dollars per day on subsidizing their agriculture, that is, six times the amount of aid they give to poor countries. In 2002 the US spent more than $3 billion on supporting its 25 000 producers of cotton, while in East Africa more than 10 million people depend on cotton production. Europe dumps its surplus dairy products, sugar and cereals in Africa, thereby taking away the livelihood of subsistence producers in that continent. On average each European cow receives a daily subsidy of $2, which is more than the daily income of hundreds of millions of poor people (Shlaes, 2003).

Moreover the strong support of agriculture in the rich countries causes serious harm to the poor countries by artificially depressing prices, which further aggravates the inequalities there. The EU Common Agricultural Policy, the provision of agricultural subsidies and non-tariff protection in the US, the escalation of corruption in weak governments – all these sully the very idea of the market economy that we preach like a faith, impose because we have the power to do so, and systematically distort to our gain.

The dismantling of protection for the economies of underdeveloped countries often causes the disappearance of structures that allowed them to survive.

The peasant economy, which involves three billion people, is now threatened in those countries which have opened themselves up to modernization. Here two phenomena play a destructive role. The first is the massive influx of agricultural products at very low prices owing to the industrialization of agriculture and the subsidies paid in rich countries, which render the small peasant farmer unable to compete. The second is the mass cultivation of crops intended for export and subject to fluctuations in the world market.

The integration of small economies into larger groups mainly benefits the more advanced partners if there is no compensating mechanism. The case of Mexico is interesting in this regard. In 1994 it entered into a free trade agreement with the US and Canada (NAFTA). The Tricontinental Centre has studied the results, which are striking (Houtart, 2002). Between 1993 and 2001 the volume of trade between the three countries almost doubled. Direct investment in the region also grew considerably. However for Mexico the consequences were mixed. While its GNP rose from $420 billion in 1994 to $574 billion in 2000, the benefits of NAFTA membership were not equally distributed and some sections of the population were adversely affected.

Three sectors were particularly hard hit: employment, agriculture and the environment. In less than 10 years 28 000 small and medium-sized businesses collapsed. During 2000 alone this meant the loss of 200 000 jobs. In parallel, subcontracting burgeoned along the border with the US, 'creating unskilled work, underpaid and characterized by often subhuman working conditions and a total unconcern for the environment' (Houtart, 2002).

Mexican agriculture has been the prime victim of the agreement. It has to compete with American productivity-focused agriculture, which also has the advantage of scale. Between 1984 and 2000 the agricultural balance fell from $581 million to minus $2.148 million. Between 1990 and 2000 imports of the 10 basic products rose from 8.7 million tons to 18.5 million tons, that is, an increase of 112 per cent. Before NAFTA came into operation imported maize amounted to 2 million tons, but by 2001 it had risen to 148 million. Of course these differences are not surprising if one knows that an American farmer generates 20 times the economic value of a Mexican farmer, that there are 1.6 tractors per worker in North America and just one for every 200 workers in Mexico, and that the annual agriculture subsidy paid to each agricultural worker is $20 000 in the US and $700 in Mexico, a difference that will be exacerbated by the farm bill that President George W. Bush pushed through in 2002.

In Mexico the massive imports drove down the value of local agricultural products, thereby impoverishing the entire peasant population. General poverty increased from 50 per cent to 52.4 per cent, and sovereignty over food production practically disappeared. Thus 'free trade between unequal partners always ends up privileging the stronger. This is not trade but domination. It is more about conquering a market and exploitation than sustainable development.' (Houtart 2002)

Yepès' (2000) study of Mexico clearly illustrates that a commercial opening up of this kind greatly increases the income divide between those who succeed in the game and those who are excluded from it. There is also a drastic reduction in the part played by and influence of local players, who have less and less of a hold on their common destiny.

The environment has also been profoundly degraded, with the subcontracting zone becoming an 'economic cesspit'.

A further example of domination concerns medicinal plants in tropical countries and the knowledge of them accumulated over the centuries by the inhabitants of these countries. Large pharmaceutical firms are determined to carry off this knowledge, patent it and exploit it on a world scale for their own gain. A vision of sustainable development would compel them to share the benefits with the countries of origin, if not to create partnerships that would foster local growth.

The absence of world governance and the pursuit of profit have also led to other types of domination and systematic destruction.

The plight of forests is well known. Uncontrolled deforestation is often carried out by large landowners who wish to develop more profitable activities such as livestock farming, undeterred by corrupt or weak governments. There is also systematic destruction of forests for their valuable timber. In many countries this activity amounts to pillage, and if there is an obligation to replant young trees it is honoured only superficially.

Overfishing, pollution of the seas by unscrupulous tanker owners, the destruction of natural habitats and the damage caused by real estate speculation are further examples of what can occur when private economic players exert their power in an irresponsible way.

Financial deviation[9]

Since 1971 the financial sector has been free from the constraints of the monetary stability imposed by the Bretton Woods Agreement. This has resulted in the establishment of a regime of floating exchange rates and, progressively, almost total freedom of the markets for money and capital. The dogmas that inspire the new system are based on the dominant ideology described earlier, and serve to strengthen it. Put simply, the dogmas are as follows:

- Capital must be able to circulate freely; the value of money is fixed by the markets.
- Balanced public budgets and price stability must be permanently maintained.

These two conditions are necessary and sufficient to ensure productive investment, growth and employment. They do not require a specific economic policy; the markets, which are efficient, can ensure equilibrium; therefore government intervention in economic matters must be kept to a minimum. It is in this spirit that the financial sector has gone global and is also becoming dominant, as Fontela (1998) has illustrated well.

World finance today consists of a global market that operates continuously. Its agents gather together all the available information on countries, firms, trade and so on. It is the financial market that puts a value on the world economy: it judges the value of the principal economic projects; it establishes what an action by a firm is worth; it judges the financial stability of governments and the interest differential to be paid to compensate for any lack of stability; it values international debts and sets the rates to be used by the players, including the national monetary authorities. This market therefore arches over all economic activities and is in a position of leadership for the evaluation and orientation of strategies for growth and development.

Of course sophisticated and globalized financial markets are indispensable to the running of a modern economy: they facilitate trade, support initiatives, organize access to capital in the best cost conditions, cover risks and so on. These roles are clearly not in question. What must be questioned is the growing imbalance between the real economy (non-financial goods and services) and the financial economy.

The provision of finance is not only a service activity. Finance is the monetary counterpart to the real activity and their mutual relationship considerably influences the way in which development is conceived and the game played. Since the financial sector has taken a dominant place and tends to impose its views on and dictate the behaviour of the real economy, the conduct of the economic system is progressively passing from entrepreneurs to financiers. As long as the latter value the firm favourably it will benefit from all the advantages of the system. If not it will run into difficulty.

As Fontela (1998) notes, the spirit of speculation tends to take precedence over the spirit of enterprise. Is this important? Yes, to the extent that the financial markets possess such power and operate on the basis of an ideology that is ill-suited to sustainable development. We shall now look at some significant aspects of this.

The financier and the entrepreneur

Inefficient financial markets

Financiers' instruments of analysis are unsuitable for a correct appreciation of the strategies of firms and the associated risks. Their information is incomplete and their financial tools are not appropriate to evaluate future projects since they are mainly based on *ex-post* results while strategic expectations are based on the information, analysis and experience of the firm, which are often of a higher standard than those of financiers. As for strategic tools, the use that the firm can make of these is generally superior to that made by the financier or external analyst. The firm is better placed to gather together and handle specific information on its customers, competitors, technology, know-how, enterprise capacity and so on. The firm is always less transparent from the outside than it is from inside.

It may be suggested that financial analysts make judgements about the future of firms that are rarely borne out by the facts, either because they overvalue them or because they undervalue them, except of course when the situation has deteriorated to the point where everyone is aware of it, like the captain who realizes his ship is sinking when the water has risen to his binoculars.

Some recent examples suggest that the ability of the financial markets to evaluate the future performance of a firm is not always based on confirmed competence or adequate objectivity.

It appears that of the some 2000 shares valued by Salomon between the early 1990s and 2001, none was recommended as a sell. And yet, of the 36 firms that the bank followed in the telecommunications sector, 16 went bankrupt between 1998 and 2002, including WorldCom and Global Crossing (Pretzlik and Silverman, 2002).

Either merchant banks are not capable of making better predictions than the public at large or, as the New York prosecutor general suggests, there is a systematic conflict of interest between the necessary rigour of the analysis and the banks' interest in gaining business from selling shares or other financial operations carried out for the firms they support. In either case the much talked-about efficiency of the financial market is called into question, and there is a danger of entrepreneurs' projects being inhibited or boosted by external analyses that undervalue or overvalue the actions of their firms.

In a period of 'irrational exuberance', completely unrealistic expectations cause a bull market, and when this collapses a recession may follow. At the time of the excitement by the American stock market for the new economy, the rumour was that Paul Volcker, former president of the Federal Reserve, would have made the following comment: 'The world economy depends on the American economy; the latter depends on the New York stock exchange, which itself depends on fifty shares of which half have not yet distributed one dollar of dividend.'

Furthermore the stock market tends to introduce a systematic distortion in the allocation of capital. In a period of growth, firms are encouraged by the financial market to increase their financial leverage, which has the result of artificially raising the profit on shares and encouraging investment in capital.

This distortion drives listed firms to overinvest in equipment and reduce their workforce in order to increase labour productivity. This is how the spiral of cost cutting is sparked off. The productivity of capital will tend to deteriorate but, as it becomes ever cheaper, this is of little importance in a period of economic expansion since labour productivity grows. The financial markets will be satisfied as long as the share price continues to rise, driven by increased demand. From this point of view it is not surprising that, in all world stock markets, shares are driven up as soon as a plan to reduce the workforce is announced.

To this is added a demand for short-term results (profitability and growth), which commits the firm to follow a path that diverges from sustainable development. When the quarterly results do not meet the market's expectations, it immediately reacts by marking down the stock. To correct this the firm often has no short-term choice but to reduce its costs.

In this way policies of permanent restructuring, transformation, regeneration, turnaround and continual cost reduction become the norm. Far from being a manifestation of the firm's creativity, these policies have the effect of magnifying the effect of so-called creative destruction. Such policies are sometimes necessary for survival but they are in no sense strategies for development and innovation. In most cases they are detrimental to the workforce and risk destroying the atmosphere and motivation required for long-term operations. In the absence of a true strategy the policies may go too far and make any development project impossible.

By excessively reducing costs the firm risks becoming anorexic, with no reserves, no dynamism and therefore in danger of losing its strategic capacity. In this case the financial sector tends to favour short-term measures over long-term projects. The requirement to announce quarterly results only emphasizes this shift.

Two essential characteristics of the collective entrepreneurial firm are threatened here: its capacity to take a long-term view of projects and its ability to convince and motivate its collaborators. If pushed too far the firm might be dehumanized, so that it ceases to be a collective venture and becomes no more than a technofinancial system devoted exclusively to generating profits.

To this must be added the perversity of a system based on share-holder value:

> The penalizing taxation of the dividend and the financial theories that propose the shareholder's remuneration by the return and appreciation have produced a system in which stock market appreciation has become an aim in itself, and the universal criterion of performance. Appreciation seems to be a blessing that would provide for everyone and cost no one. During the years that the stock markets were running high, public opinion and the markets closed their eyes if the CEOs and their banker friends who were said to be the source of this appreciation took their share on the way, a share whose considerable size has several disadvantages: it made hosts of CEOs and bankers lose their sense of ethics; it was the motivation for baseless mergers and acquisitions; it progressively corrupted the other financial markets and led to generalized cupidity. (de Keuleneer, 2003)

The enterprise becomes a good

Financial capitalism often leads to raids on and hostile acquisitions of firms with a view to selling them off piecemeal in order to make a profit on the stock market. This was the case with the huge wave of hostile takeovers in the 1970s, when the spirit of speculation clearly triumphed over the will for enterprise. The initiators of these takeovers got the names they deserved: sharks, predators, raiders. For example the raid on Firestone prompted a barrage of criticism by society and the town in which Firestone was situated was threatened with losing its main economic base.

During the same period British American Tobacco was subject to a raid by a group of financiers who criticized it for being too diversified. They wanted to dismantle the firm and sell off everything that was not related to tobacco. The head of the firm justified the diversification by saying that sales of tobacco were likely to go down in the developed countries; moreover this activity presented a moral problem. The raiders' reply was clear: the developing countries have a growing population – concentrate on them.

This was a purely financial view of the firm. It was no longer a living organization or a source of collective creativity, just a set of more or less profitable assets that could be bought and sold in the market. 'It must be noted that ... hostile acquisitions have paid scant attention to the human and social reality of the firm which comes to be the target, then the prey of a takeover' (Cobbaut, 1997).

This view of the firm as a profit centre, rather than an entity with synergetic elements, opened the way to all kinds of speculative operation. A recent example was the purchase by an American financial group of a German firm manufacturing submarines (Howaldtswerke Deutsche Werft). This took place in 2002; in 2003 it was put up for sale because of an error in forecasting its results. The enterprise as merchandise! 'a company director is not a fund manager. He depends on the loyalty of customers and staff. Managing companies is not about mergers and acquisitions and disposals but about running operating business well' (Kay, 2002).

Acquisitions and friendly mergers have also figured in strategies over the past 20 years. These serve quite different purposes: external growth as a substitute for internal growth and to accelerate development strategies.

Here the strategic motivation is twofold: evaluation of the possible synergies, and the price that the buyer is willing to pay. Such acquisitions and mergers are often financed by shares and are therefore based on the value assessed by market financiers. In general, upon the announcement of an operation of this kind the buyer's shares tend to go down and those of the seller rise. The offer is often raised and the higher bids can reach unreasonable levels.

Few acquisitions/mergers are completely successful; many fail, causing erosion of value. Here the speculation comes more from the entrepreneur than from the financier, but this type of operation may also treat the firm like a good, and when it fails there is a loss of essential resources for development: motivated managers, loyal customers, collective capacity, investment savings and so on.

It should be stressed that the regulations governing these operations are essentially financial: they are concerned to put all shareholders on the same footing. They are not concerned with the quality of the strategic approach, the frenzy of possible overbids or social consequences. Again, the firm as merchandise!

We must also mention the fragility of the empires built on sand that financial capitalism facilitates, including Vivendi, Kirche, Maxwell and the recent ventures outside the traditional domains, such as bank assurance (Allianz-Dresdner Bank) and mobile telephony.

Today John Maynard Keynes' 'casino economy' has a variant: the 'monopoly economy'. This can only be beneficial if it is integrated into a serious-minded strategy, guided by a sense of responsibility towards all groups involved (the stakeholders). In other words, mergers and acquisitions risk being destructive rather than creative if they do not fit into a programme of sustainable development.

Monetary fluctuations and entrepreneurial strategies

From the global point of view, monetary stability is no longer assured and this is one of the major defects of the current system.

From the point of view of the firm, the international competitive game is made more difficult and dangerous by currency volatility – the best strategies can be foiled by monetary fluctuations. That is why many firms put considerable energy into financial games that shelter them from such risks or may, through speculative activities, increase profits.

One has only to think of the growth in off-balance-sheet activities, the increasing importance to the firm of the financial manager and his or her team, and the development of financial and fiscal engineering. Note also that a section of derivative products is aimed at skirting regulations and avoiding taxation.

To the extent that the profitability of the firm depends on this type of activity, it may be suggested once again that finance prevails over the main activity and that here too the spirit of speculation outstrips the spirit of enterprise.

As a footnote we can add that deregulation has weakened and reduced the coherence of financial structures:

> Subject to strong constraint to sell loans in order to preserve their market share, the banks show themselves to be incapable of evaluating risks correctly. Examples abound: the excessive third world debt, a consequence of the constraint of recycling petro-dollars, the collapse of junk bonds, the cataclysm of the American savings banks. (Cobbaut, 1997)

To this is added the systemic risk caused by the development of derivative products.

The damaging effects of an excessive monetarism

As Fontela (1998) shows, an excess of monetary orthodoxy (price stability) and budgetary rigour can cause central banks and international institutions to implement restrictive economic policies. If taken too far these can provoke deflation.

After the Second World War, in the framework of the Bretton Woods Agreement, the advanced countries experienced years of exceptional growth. In France they have been called the 30 glorious years. During this period capital movements were controlled, interest rates were low and inflation under control. Monetary policies followed the needs of the real economy and a spirit of enterprise prevailed over the spirit of speculation. This rapid growth and other factors caused inflation, which risked undermining the advantages gained. The response was radical. Under the influence of the Chicago School of economists the vision of development was inverted: in order to curb inflation it was no longer necessary to stimulate global demand but to implement a supply-side policy that encouraged competitiveness and innovation.

There developed what Fontela (1998) calls a pessimistic vision of the world. One passed 'from the anticipations of growth in the research into price stability, from the acceptance of imbalances as a source of progress to the recommendation of equilibrium as the sole acceptable situation'. This once again arises from the *single thought* mistaking means for ends, useful means that become dangerous it they turn to be too absolute.

This perspective is very visible today in Europe, where firms are 'ready to exchange growth and employment for an improvement in monetary stability and budgetary equilibrium' (Fontela, 1995). Fontela sees this as being responsible for persistent unemployment and the 'missed opportunities' of sustained growth. In his eyes the EU has not yet succeeded in producing true growth from the creation of the single market, and Germany has not been able to gain from its reunification or from opening up to the east in order to stimulate its growth and reduce its unemployment.

The mandate of the European Central Bank (ECB) goes in this direction. It is strengthened by the Stability Pact, which restricts governments' scope for economic action. In fact the EU monetary policy and the fiscal policies of member-state governments have not only become more rigid but they are also uncoordinated.

To ensure its credibility the ECB imposes a restrictive and uniform monetary policy (one size fits all). Fiscal policies are all that remain to member-state governments that wish to stimulate or restrain their economies. The budgetary rigour imposed on them by the Stability Pact has removed a large part of their power to act. Moreover the individual economies are increasingly dependent on an unsubtle monetarism.

Some economists see potential disasters in this, others think that it is a necessary condition for the stability of the single market. In any event the approach has not yet succeeded in creating an environment that is favourable to expansion. The unemployment and weak growth experienced in the EU are at least partial consequences of this. It is not only the lack of 'flexibility' of the labour market that, as the believers in the 'single thought' claim, explain its relative economic stagnation.

In defence of monetarism, some cite the recent history of the US economy and its uninterrupted growth until 2001. However one should not be taken in by this or put it down to the sole application of monetarist rules. In the US monetary and fiscal policies are much better coordinated than in the EU, budgetary deficits have been frequent and widely accepted, an enormous imbalance exists in the balance of payments, and above all the spirit of enterprise and innovation has prevailed in the case of the new technologies, creating a wave of growth.

A true strategy for sustainable development will not emerge just from monetary, financial and fiscal policies but also from a more subtle, dynamic and less prescribed mix of tools for and stimuli of balanced growth: well-tempered use of the market and competition (Adam Smith 1930), creativity and innovation (Schumpeter 1949), stimulation of demand and the pursuit of full employment (Keynes 1936).

In the developing countries, monetarism is not only deflationary it could also be destructive. The IMF and World Bank are profoundly imbued with the ideology of unconditional opening up of markets and budgetary rigour. Their systems of loans and aid are conditioned by this model. They work on the outdated hypothesis that the market spontaneously achieves the most effective results. They forget the asymmetries of power and the phenomenon of domination.

In a recent book Stiglitz (2002), former vice-president of the World Bank, criticizes the exaggerated monetarism of these institutions. Without denying that they have often brought real help to many countries, he condemns the ideology that governs their interventions and is beginning to have a negative effect on millions of poor people. The conditions for development aid have become draconian: liberalization of the capital market, which imposes high rates of interest; commercial opening up without regard for nascent industrialization and without the establishment of an adequate social security system; non-intervention by the state in certain national projects; and the obligation to repay loans within the deadline and according to pre-scribed conditions.

To accelerate liberalization the IMF and World Bank demand the adoption of adjustment policies in budgetary and fiscal matters, thereby imposing a deflationary bias that pushes many countries into poverty and chaos. In some cases these policies have caused famines and riots, and the rigid rules on debt repayment have necessitated large cuts in the budgets for education, health and security.

The monetarist policies have thus produced a situation that is quite opposite to that intended, namely balanced and sustainable development. Austerity has been imposed without political debate and without consensus on or national support for a long-term project for change: 'The tone is that of a colonial master' (ibid.). The international institutions have become 'dominant players, dominated by the rich countries and commercial interests. They see the world with the eyes of the financial community' (ibid.). This is a dramatic illustration of the financial shift we are discussing here.

Prasad *et al.*'s (2003) study of the opening up of these countries to the movement of capital shows that this is unfavourable if they do not have strong financial institutions and honest governments. If these two conditions are not met their integration into the global capital market assures neither growth nor macroeconomic stability. Financial globalization can only benefit them once a particular institutional and political threshold has been crossed, but the acceleration of competition and the policies of international institutions often force them to open up and liberalize before these conditions exist.

We should add that the World Bank has for a long time refused to concern itself with the existence of corruption on the pretext that this does not come within its mandate. This position is beginning to change thanks to strong personalities such as the current president of the World Bank and certain NGOs, such as Transparency International (Eigen, 2003).

Behavioural deviation

Behavioural deviations include excesses, lies and trickery. They are often induced by the systemic and financial deviations discussed above. But they are also the result of human weakness, and realism obliges us to recall that they are not new and we do not live in a perfect world.[10] Whatever the characteristics of a more sustainable and humane development model, it must be accepted that blunders will always occur. This is the price of freedom and the product of human passions.

One should add that such excesses are relatively rare and are often punished. The majority of economic players are honest at the individual level. One should not inflate the recent scandals to the point of presenting them as typical of current practices in economic life.

These deviations were doubtless less dangerous than the preceding ones, which were rooted in the system itself. In the US, however, recent scandals have led Americans to wonder whether these were simply due to the moral weakness of some managers or, more profoundly, whether these are defects in the capitalist system.

One could suggest that, to the extent that the system is poorly regulated and the spirit of speculation is dominant, there is a risk that the defects will broaden and behavioural deviations will increase. The risk is all the greater when the instrumental logic that tends make profit an end in itself does not offer alternative values and aims that will allow people to resist the temptation of money.

When the excesses are committed by players who possess great economic power the consequences can be quite negative. In a world that is becoming more complex and interdependent the stakes are becoming higher.

Below we shall provide a few illustrations. These do not cover the whole range of deviant practices; they are simply intended to show the types of thing that can occur if a development model is too exclusively guided by a single thought, without purpose other than the competitiveness of markets or a benchmark other than profitability. The examples will also provide an understanding of the vigour of some reactions and the moral disrepute that might spread throughout the system.

Product deception

The most visible and scandalous case in this respect is that of the tobacco industry. For 50 years firms in this sector have conspired to conceal the life-threatening and addictive nature of their products.[11] The US Attorney-General, Janet Reno, has spoken at length on the actions of which they are accused:

> launching a conspiracy to deceive the public about the risks of cancer caused by tobacco... conducting their business without regard for the truth, the law, the health of the American people... campaigning to preserve their enormous profits whatever the cost in human lives, in suffering and in medical expenditure... organizing a public relations campaign to create a false debate on these points... lying about the dependency of the smoker with regard to tobacco... recruiting new smokers among children in order to replace those who died. (Reno, 1997)

The firms in question defended themselves in terms of instrumental economic logic (the importance of the sector for employment, external trade and so on) or fiscal contributions: the treasury obtains considerable revenues from these products. Little or nothing was said about values or ethics. Among a number of judicial rulings one involved a fine of $250 billion, to be paid over 25 years. (Master Settlement Agreement with 50 US states, 1998). In 2004, the US Department of Justice used anti-racketeering legislation to press its claim that cigarette manufacturers colluded to keep smokers hooked. The action is being brought under the 1970 Racketeer Influenced and Corrupt Organization Act, designed to fight organized crime. 'The government's primary allegation is that the US Tobacco Industry was essentially one illegal enterprise just like the mafia,' says Martin Feldman, tobacco analyst at Merrill Lynch. The government says the defendants should 'disgorge', or forfeit $280 billion of 'ill-gotten' gains (Buckley, 2004).

This example shows the extremes brought about by an ethical shift in a system that has no other purpose than its own growth. Other less serious and less systematic examples may be cited.

Some merchant banks, caught in a conflict of interests between their roles as financial analysts and providers of services, have been accused of deceiving investors about the value of the firms with which they deal. In the past this conflict of interests was resolved by the 'Chinese wall' that was supposed to exist between the two roles. Ostensibly analysts did not have contact with other departments of the bank and could value firms in an independent manner. They were not supposed to help their colleagues increase their turnover from the firms they were valuing.

In 2002 the Financial Services Committee of the US Congress held an enquiry into the possible existence of illegal practices aimed at undervaluing or overvaluing share prices at the time of issue on the New York stock exchange. This practice would create considerable financial advantages for the directors of the issuing firm and enable its bank to secure the business of handling issues or the provision of other financial services. An American prosecutor is currently investigating whether, in a number of cases, there has been a conspiracy between certain groups of investors, banks' financial analysts and client firms to swindle individual investors out of hundreds of millions of dollars. The facts have yet to be established, but the very possibility of such deception shows that the system must be reformed.

In a similar vein, a large American bank has been accused by investors and the control authorities of making exaggeratedly positive stock recommendations to the public with the aim of winning over firms and thus securing contracts for share issues or advice. A prosecutor has produced a treasure trove of evidence that reveals a shocking contrast between the bank's official recommendations and the private comments of its best analyst.

The bank's constant advice was 'buy or accumulate for the short or long term'. The analyst's private comments about the shares were 'this stock is a load of rubbish, there is nothing that will put the firm on its feet in the short term'.

Another example is that of pharmaceutical firms concealing the inadequacy of drug trials or the possible dangers of a product.

We can also cite the weapons industry, whose activities are often ambiguous, divided between the service of defence and more or less secret sales to the belligerents of civil wars or cruel ethnic conflicts. In this domain the deception is less to do with the product than with its destination.

Deception in the figures

Scandals involving fraudulent accounting and financial dishonesty have received widespread attention. Large and small deceptions of this nature are not new. There have always been accounting manipulations, fiscal fraud, the corruption of officials and the payment of kickbacks. Once again, these are part and parcel of the imperfections of mankind and its systems. Of course attempts must be made to contain these within the tightest boundaries, but they will always be there.

From 2000 in the US a series of scandals was made public. The majority of these involved a manipulation of accounts that went well beyond the limits of what is referred to as creative accounting or fiscal engineering: concealment of debts in independent subsidiaries, inclusion of future profits in current accounts, conversion of capital expenditure, invention of fictitious customers, inflation of incomes and profits and so on.

In some cases these manipulations resulted in large personal gains for executives via loans, exaggerated remuneration, stock manipulations, insider dealings and so on. Other deceptions involved theft, perjury and the destruction of documents.

Prestigious names such as Enron, Andersen, WorldCom and Tyco were heaped with opprobrium and for a while it was thought that confidence in the system might be undermined. The public authorities reacted quickly and took draconian measures to ensure control and transparency, as well as inflicting heavy punishments.

What is interesting for our argument is the spirit revealed by this trickery. It was the enterprise culture that made it possible, and this again draws attention to the dangers of a system that lacks clear aims. It was a response to the possibility of easy money and reflected a lack of restraint, even honesty, at a time of market excitement.

The emergence of the new economy, with its fabulous promises, gave rise to stock exchange euphoria. This wave of optimism accelerated into a chain of events that led, from the end of the 1990s, to the creation of a bubble and its collapse (Moises, 2002). First, there was easy access to capital for firms that were selling the dream: information technology and communication, the internet and virtual society, the biotechnologies.

Then there was the difficulty of understanding and valuing the growing importance of such intangible resources as technology, patents, software, brands and the rapidly developing derivative products.

Finally, grafted onto all this was an undeniable spirit of enterprise (great innovations had been made), but also a desire for personal gain and wealth, which seemed easy to attain and without limit: high pay, bonuses, stock options and other stock exchange benefits were possible in the time of the booming bull market.

This put the system under pressure and boosting share values became a major objective, not only for shareholders but also for those executives whose accumulation of wealth depended on it. It was then that the dishonest behaviour took place: 'nothing puts reason to sleep more than vast amounts on money obtained without effort'.[12]

What should be emphasized here is the development of a totally immoral corporate culture. There was a climate of gain and speculation in firms whose orientation was exclusively financial and whose activities were directed at short-term growth in stock value. The majority of these were new enterprises that lacked an ethical tradition and whose mentality was often that of nouveaux riches intoxicated by new-found fortune. An analysis of the firms where the major scandals occurred clearly reveals a 'reckless and ruthless' culture.[13] Attention was focused solely on pushing up the share value by any means, whether risky or plain dishonest. Those who played this game were handsomely rewarded. Those who had doubts or raised objections were persecuted or sacked. Objectors or whistle-blowers were rare and did not last long in their firms, which continued their dubious practices unobserved.

All of this resulted in an institutional arrogance, a cult of new 'winners', the too-rapid promotion of young 'stars' and those devoted to the boss, and in the intimidation of those who dared to question this type of behaviour.

In one case 'a small group of executives was in a position to milk the firm to the detriment of thousands of its employees' (*Financial Times*, 9 April 2002). Corruption went right through the firm and involved a large number of managers. Enron was dubbed the 'crooked E' because the swindling was so widespread. It was discovered that the 144 most senior managers had received $744 million from the firm in the year before its collapse. This figure was ten times the amount allocated to compensate the 4500 employees who lost their jobs due to the bankruptcy. This pillage of the organization's resources was governed by dominant and intimidating personalities. Their concept of power was to impose unilateral views, to ignore the opinions of others and to champion the 'star system'.

Such cases are interesting for two reasons. First, they illustrate how morality can be abandoned when the pursuit of profit is pushed to the limit. Second, they enable a comparison of two cultures: one in which the spirit of speculation dominates, and one in which the spirit of enterprise still reigns. In general, firms that were more traditional and oriented towards products, customers and strategies for development escaped the wave of scandals. But even among those firms, as in all human affairs, there were borderline cases. The case of Shell is interesting in this respect. The scandal of overestimating its oil reserves stemmed more, it seems, from the ambition of a director than from the culture of a firm. Clearly one cannot compare Shell to Enron. Even if its credibility has been reduced, its will to promote sustainable development cannot called into question by an individual deception that has been recognized and corrected.

It could be suggested that the cultural element is an essential constituent of a model of sustainable development, and that the culture of the entrepreneur is much closer to the concept of the responsible firm than is a more financial and speculative culture.

Hubris, short-sightedness and indifference

Power that is overpersonalized can lead to excesses: excessive centralization, failure to listen or delegate, a court like climate of intrigue, and excesses in terms of strategic ambitions, future projects, diversification, poorly planned acquisitions and empires built too quickly.

Examples abound of strategies adopted by a 'heroic leader' and that arose more from a bet or from over optimism than from economic reasoning.

Vivendi was a recent and obvious case in 1994. At the age of 34 Jean-Marie Messier was appointed as head of Générale des Eaux, a large and respectable water distribution firm. He was young, dynamic, ambitious and persuasive. He put forward a new vision of the future of the firm: to become a world communications group.[14] This project was interesting and the personality behind it was exciting from many points of view. But the basic idea was very general: the twentieth century was the era of industry, the twenty-first would be that of services, particularly those stimulated and supported by the new technologies. Communication, like water, was a service and there might be certain complementarities between the two.

Like many others Messier believed there to be a synergy between content (music, films, TV programmes) and its distribution (broadcasting, mobile phones, the Internet and so on). For example he seemed to be convinced that he would be able to persuade millions of consumers to pay to receive such contents on third-generation mobile phones (3G).

He began his empire building by buying Seagram, the alcoholic drinks giant and owner of an important company in music and films (Universal). The sums involved were considerable: the purchase of Seagram cost £34 billion, while the sale of numerous activities that did not fit in with project (property, public works, clinics, student restaurants) brought in $22 billion. The latter was immediately reinvested in new acquisitions: Havas, Canal+, Cogetel and Pathé.

In four years Messier put together the world's second communications group, playing at the 'court of the great' like AOL-Time Warner and Disney. There were 381 000 employees, the turnover in 2001 was $58 billion and the group's activities were divided equally between water treatment and communication (music, films, publishing, telecommunications, internet). At its peak the share value was $150. Two years later it fell by $17.8 and Messier goes and his successor starts to dismantle the group. What happened? A return to the boom and bust of the bubble? Yes. Personal quarrels between executives and shareholders? Yes. Loss of confidence in Messier? Definitely. But these were not the heart of the problem, which without doubt lay in hubris and excess.

Was it not excessive to believe that by buying and selling firms it would be possible to construct a durable and solid empire in four years?

Was it reasonable to start from a core business based on water supply to diversify into communication?

Could the will of a single man, his dynamism, intelligence and energy be sufficient to develop synergy, teamwork and the necessary motivation to transform miscellaneous groups into a successful corporation? The costume of Harlequin often becomes a Nessus tunic that destroys the person who wears it. The development of the company was far from the cumulative process of progress gained from knowledge of the business, a common culture, a shared vision and patient construction of an international strategic capacity.

A headlong race cannot take the place of systematic strategic development. Positive media coverage may be convincing for a while, but this cannot create true synergy, cooperation among organizations and collective development.

Was there not excess in this voluntarism, in the announcement of the end of French cultural products' exclusion from the free trade provisions of the WTO, in the adoption of the 'star system'?

This case was not unique. In the same sector the dream of AOL-Time Warner to build a universal multimedia empire by combining content with distribution turned into dust for the same reasons: synergy cannot be improvised, voluntarism is not enough, and it is very difficult to make a success of acquisitions, mergers and diversification.

The 'heroic' leaders who sparked the new technology bubble often lacked the necessary objectivity and modesty to build large organizations.[15] One should not confuse entrepreneurs with adventurers.

Another illustration of excess is provided by the rewards, sometimes outrageous, given to executives. In 1970, on average the heads of

American firms earned 25 times more than workers; in 2000 they earned 600 times more. Today, even after the drop in the value of options, they still earn 300 times more (Skapinker, 2003). In Europe the gap is much smaller.

In the US, an enquiry into the rewards received by 181 executives and directors of 25 large firms that went bankrupt after 1 January 2001 revealed that during the two previous years these people had earned $3.3 billion in pay, bonuses and the sale of shares and options. During the same period and for the same firms close on 100 000 workers lost their jobs and the shareholders lost more than $200 billion (*Financial Times*, 31 July, 1–2 August 2003 and Cheng 2003).

The individual figures for the period are staggering. At the top of the list, Garry Winnick, head of Global Crossing, cleared $512 million, (salary, bonus and other cash plus gross share sales), Ken Lay of Enron $247 million, (gross share sales + identifiable option profits) (Betts, 2002) with the remainder ranging from $270 to $37 million, taking into account stock options. Bernie Ebbers, the former head of WorldCom, received a bonus of $10 million for remaining at least two years in the company (retention fee). The payment of $139.5 million to Richard Grasso, president of the New York Stock Exchange as miscellaneous compensation is another example (Glassman, 2003).

Some cases exist in Europe as well. The pension plan and other benefit payments awarded in 1997 as a tax-free lump sum to Percy Barnevik, the respected head of ABB, the Swiss-Swedish engineering group, amounted to $100 million (SFr 148 millions). Mr Jacob Wallenberg, ABB board member, declared this was 'wholly unreasonable' Shareholders were kept in the dark. According to ABB's vice-chairman no one in the supervisory board knew about this payement (Brown-Humes and Hall, 2002). In 2002, to put an end to the controversy about this matter, Mr Barnevik gave up more than half of his pension and severance benefits.

The severance compensation provided for Jean-Marie Messier and under discussion in 2003 was $20.6 million (Johnson, 2003).

The severance compensation offered to M. Esser, the head of Mannesmann, allegedly to persuade him to withdraw his opposition to the company's purchase by Vodafone, amounted to $30 million (combining contractual severance pay and a appreciation award) while paying at the same time $44 million to other Mannesmann management board members (Jenkins, 2004; Barber and Benoit, 2002).

Sums of this nature obviously arise from a mentality of easy wealth, and reflect the triumph of an unregulated financial approach in which the spirit of cupidity prevails over the spirit of enterprise and, in the case of bankruptcy, completely destroys it.

One understands the fury felt by employees who have lost their jobs and often part of their pension when they learn of the outrageous sums paid to the 'barons of bankruptcy' or for abortive ventures.

Political short-sightedness is another consequence of the 'single thought'. For example when South Africa wanted to fight AIDS by copying and transforming into generic products the sophisticated and very expensive drugs produced by the large pharmaceutical firms, the latter brought an action against South Africa on the legitimate (in their eyes) ground of protecting their patents. Their argument was that research would have to stop if drugs could not be protected by patent for a sufficiently long time to recoup the sums expended on research and development. (Although based on a legal plane, political negotiation proved possible and specific arrangements were made.)

How could companies be so insensitive to the social and ethical aspects of an illness that is ravaging poor countries and causing more damage there than anywhere else, as to deal with this question via the courts? To be fair it must be added that not all business leaders are so insensitive. For example the Bill and Melinda Gates Foundation, which has been set up to fight AIDS in poor countries, is an impressive sign of compassion about human suffering.

Instrumental logic not only makes one short-sighted, it also makes one blind. Under the pressure of public opinion the firms in question were persuaded to adopt a more diplomatic approach. 'In a struggle between you and the world, put your money on the world' (Kafka, quoted in de Brabandère, 1998).

*   *   *

Our development model is becoming unsustainable. If we do not quickly reform it we risk growing imbalances and unprecedented catastrophes.

The system is going off course. Its acceleration is threatening the planet and destabilizing its inhabitants. Excessive market orientation is leaving the weakest by the roadside. The law of the market is permeating everything. Audience ratings and advertising are dictating our lifestyle, education and culture. The world of finance and the spirit of speculation are contaminating economic activity and encouraging excesses, with ever worsening consequences.

To close our eyes to this is to confine ourselves to the single thought, which is unworthy of a citizen. To make no effort to remedy it smacks of irresponsibility, the egoism of the well-off or the hypocrisy of the cynic. Some people are beginning to object and to call into question a system that no longer has any clear aims.

Can any firm that claims to be responsible bury its head in the sand in the face of these deviations and threats? On the pretext of an economic logic that has been imposed upon it, can it refuse to enter resolutely into an ethical and political debate with a view to trans-forming the system?

We have arrived at a decisive moment: it is still possible to reform and fundamentally improve things – let us not fail. Those who possess economic and technical power certainly cannot take on everything, but in a world of technoscience they have a major role to play. This is the subject of the second part of this book.

Periods of transition are always difficult. As Gramsci (1970) said: 'The old dies, the new does not yet see the day. In this interregnum monsters rise up.' These monsters are already visible: widespread poverty, ethnic conflict, the destruction of resources and biodiversity, cloning, genetic manipulation and so on.

Are we not losing our senses? Is it not madness to lock oneself into a single thought and to believe in it? What is this world that 'people do not eat meat for fear of becoming mad, dare not make love for fear of becoming ill and no longer press an aerosol button for fear of having the sky fall on their head'? (Latour, 1999).

In the developed world, refusal to see combined with illusion and indifference are only too evident. It is another form of madness. As Erasmus put it, 'There is a lunacy that the Furies unleash from Hell, every time that they send in their serpents and inflame the hearts of mortals with war and the unquenchable thirst for gold ... The other madness is nothing like it ... It emerges every time that a gentle illusion frees the soul from its painful cares.'

Part II

New Corporate Culture and Sustainable Development

Introduction

But if there is a sense of what is real . . . there must be something that one might call the sense of the possible . . . a flight of fancy, a will to build, a conscious utopia which, far from fearing reality, treats it simply as a task and a perpetual reinvention (Robert Musil, 1957).

In the face of criticism of the development model and calls for its transformation, many economists and business people reply that the criticisms are perhaps true, but what can replace an economic system that we know to be the only effective one?

This book suggests that it is less a question of changing the mechanics of the system and risking the loss of its creativity than of persuading those who pursue it to go beyond the means and address the ends. It is less a question of transforming its structures than of changing its culture and, through that, some orientations.

What we propose for the firm can be summarized as follows:

- Broaden the firm's *raison d'être*, that is, pay more attention to the aims and purpose of its activities and focus on its role in progress, rather than reducing everything to the financial dimension. This will allow the firm to explore its ethical and civic dimension by questioning the meaning of its actions: economic and technical progress for what? For whom? How?

  The firm can then shed its purely instrumental logic and integrate its operations into the broader vision of human progress and general interest. In a globalizing economy, answering the above questions cannot be confined to the addressing of means. Rather it is necessary to rethink the purpose of the firm and redefine its *raison d'être*.

- Develop an ethics for the future. This involves going beyond the question of integrity and posing the real question of our era: what kind of world do we wish to build together? This will enable the firm to place at the core of its principles for action values that are capable of shedding moral light on its strategic choices and social behaviour and on the new problems of our time.

- Engage in greater consultation with the new players of the globalizing world. By extending its political culture the responsible firm will be open to debate if its actions could have major social consequences. To the traditional methods of consultation with social partners will be added dialogue with other representatives of civil society at the international level.

• Position its plans for progress in a model of sustainable development. This concept is beginning to be refined and to become a conceptual and political reality. Firms can decisively contribute to its implementation through their capacity for action.

As can be seen, we are not proposing a ready-made economic model that is radically different, but a dynamic process of improving and transforming the existing model. This should make it possible to correct the unfavourable dimensions of that model while safeguarding its dynamism and creativity.

Firms are used to change and renewal. They are capable of innovating in the domain of social responsibilities, just as they continually do in the commercial sphere in order to stay in the race. By adopting a proactive attitude, the most enlightened of them can show that such a development is possible.

Of course firms alone will not be able to transform the development model. National and international public authorities, other social players, teaching institutions and the financial markets will also have to play a part. But the firm, as the principal agent of the economic system, can exert a decisive influence.

6
Broadening the *Raison d'être* of the Firm

> *All techniques look after one aspect of reality or of life but not after the orientation of life.*
>
> (Plato)
>
> *Never forget where the path leads.*
>
> (Heraclitus)

'The social responsibility of the firm is to maximize profit for the shareholder.' This famous statement by Milton Friedman, winner of the Nobel Prize for economics, has profoundly influenced neoliberal thought. Today we must try to escape from this restricted view.

Some firms are attempting to do this by broadening their sense of responsibility to include all those who have an interest or a stake: the stakeholders. This move is in the right direction and has the advantage of being practical, but it is too limited. The financial markets take little account of it and their pressure for profit maximization remains intense.

Moreover the approach is too contingent and pragmatic to facilitate the definition of a new purpose for the firm and enable it to regain its social and political legitimacy. More enlightened leaders are trying to establish a balance between all the interests involved and to sell this to financial analysts. But the actual purpose of their action is not sufficiently explicit and the development model is still overly governed by the requirement to maximize profit. This is particularly true in the Anglo-Saxon countries and Europe is falling into step with them. The same applies to the majority of management schools.

If firms are to integrate with the community and take responsibility for the social consequences of their actions, they will have to redefine their *raison d'être* and their role in an economic system that is off course and in which they are the principal players.

This system is only an element of a much larger one. Since the time of Aristotle the European tradition has been for economics, ethics and politics to form part of a single entity (European Commission, 2001). Economics is only a subsystem, and by restricting the aim of the firm simply to financial success, its civic dimension is eliminated. By not making it focus more on the general interest there is a danger of it losing its legitimacy.

In our complex world, and because of the deviations inherent in the current economic model, entrepreneurial dynamism and the common good are not automatically linked. Autonomous economic growth, disconnected from pressing political and social problems, can have unacceptable consequences. Hence the pursuit of profit can no longer be the exclusive purpose of the firm, as advocated by Milton Friedman and his disciples.

Taking into account their power for action and the social conse-quences of their strategies, firms must look beyond profit and explicitly consider the general interest. They must act in the long-term interest of the common good, which market forces do not entirely define.

The theme of general interest goes well beyond the firm. The latter can only contribute to it on the basis of its specific function, which is of an economic and technical nature. The extent to which its actions may affect society must determine its assumption of responsibility since, to reiterate, in these days of globalization there is no automatic link between the pursuit of profit and the general interest.

Claiming that it is sufficient for the firm to pursue its own logic as the state will look after the rest is an irresponsible attitude that stems from an outdated ideology and excessive belief in the effectiveness of the state and the efficiency of the market.

The specific function of the firm

In order to tackle the difficult question of the purpose of the firm, it is useful to divide the analysis into three parts and investigate the entrepreneurial action, its results and its uniqueness. Entrepreneurial actions are defined in terms of initiative, dynamism and innovation.

Based on identified needs, embarking on an undertaking consists of the following:

- Bringing together, renewing or creating the necessary resources.
- Directing these towards the needs of the market and continually reorienting them according to changes in demand and changing technologies.
- Using them in the most productive manner by adapting them to the actions of competitors and technical progress.

Of course this assumes that the mechanisms of the market and competition operate as expected, economic creativity is able to develop with sufficient freedom and flexibility and the state is able to ensure that the rules of the game are adhered to.

The result of this dynamic action is the creation of a product or a service that will be profitable if the process has been conducted in a proper manner.

It is important to stress that goods become a material reality before becoming a financial reality: goods are produced, needs are satisfied, progress is achieved, people's living standards may improve and the region in question may develop. In the process jobs have been created, supply and distribution networks have been put in place, salaries have been paid and so on. We shall return later to the negative aspects of 'creative destruction', whose effects are real rather than financial. Here we emphasize that the function of enterprise cannot be reduced to mere profit, or to the analysis of a balance sheet or profit and loss account.

In order to survive and be profitable in normal conditions of competition, an entrepreneurial undertaking must result in advancement at the technical, economic and organizational levels. In addition to their simple function of producing goods or services, firms must innovate in order to bring about material progress, as represented by the advancement from the stagecoach to the high-speed train, from the abacus to the adding machine and the computer, from the telegraph to e-mail and the internet. At the societal and financial levels, advancement is reflected in the lowering of prices and distribution of the instruments of modern life, leisure and health; greater satisfaction of the needs of customers; an increase in individuals' buying power;

growth in society's capacity for action and the wherewithal for continued economic development.

Successful firms create a surplus, an added value, an increase in goods and services. This surplus is at the heart of economic development. Thus firms promote progress and create profit. The latter is the financial side of the surplus, progress is the real side. From this point of view, profit is the result of the mastery of creativity and productivity. It is the reward, the recompense for the progress made, which requires vision, authority, effort and a taste for risk-taking.

It is also the precondition for future progress since it provides the firm with the necessary resources to pursue its strategy. Concrete progress is what gives profit its soundest justification.

Profit fulfils three important functions: it is the test of the firm's economic performance and it measures the way in which it achieves its specific function; it covers the risks that this function causes the firm to take in an unpredictable competitive world; it remunerates the shareholders and provides finance for the tangible and intangible investments that are necessary to maintain the firm's creativity.

Viewed in this way, reducing the actions of entrepreneurs and the initiative, innovation and material progress that go with them to mere financial results and shareholder value smacks of conceptual short-sightedness. Numerous researchers have shown that the most successful firms consider profit to be more a result than an end in itself. For them, what counts is progress, innovation and customer satisfaction (see in particular Collins and Porras, 1994; Lambin and Chumpitaz, 2004; de Woot and Desclée, 1984).

Is there perhaps a touch of hair-splitting in separating the concept of progress from that of profit? Is this not merely a question of semantics? I do not believe so, because by just talking about a firm's profitability one is locking the discussion into an instrumental logic.

As for the question 'profit for what?', the answer can only be to make the shareholder richer or to make more profit tomorrow. On the other hand the question 'progress for what?' obliges us to enter into the realm of aims and to debate the purpose of economic and technical progress, which is precisely the aim of this book. The answers to this question must be ethically and politically oriented, whereas the profit approach isolates the firm from society and absolves it from discussing and questioning the meaning of its actions.

If we want to define the responsibilities of the firm, we must rely on a concept that describes its function in terms that are real rather than financial.

Economic and technical progress provides the cornerstone of reflection on the purpose of economic action. In the market economy the firm is the agent of this progress. As we have seen, its function is not only to produce goods and services but also to ensure their adaptation in a climate of innovation and creativity. It is the firm that achieves this progress and brings it into its most concrete form. It does not simply perceive or describe it, it also creates and carries it out.

This concept allows us to identify the specific contribution that the firm makes to society, the function that it alone is capable of fulfilling and that differentiates it from other organizations, such as the government, unions, universities, NGOs and so on.

With this approach, enterprise is not reduced to the individual aims of the players – shareholders or stakeholders such as employees, managers, customers, suppliers and so on (Freeman, 1984) – as that would result only in the sum of quite disparate interests.

Moreover the specific role of the firm must not be confused with the common good. It does not cover the whole field of general interest. Economic and technical progress is only one, although important, aspect of a more complete human progress that also includes culture, politics, education and social justice. Therefore the firm's precise function has to be positioned within the larger entity of the common good of a society that is undergoing globalization.

Behind the somewhat abstract concept of material progress there is a complex and fragile blend of human commitments and qualitative realities. This is what one could refer to as creativity.

Collective and individual entrepreneurs have an intangible dimension that eludes quantitative analysis or political voluntarism and whose features are vision, risk taking and facing up to uncertainty; networks, relationships, tensions and efforts; the patient building up of diversified organizations, competent teams and leadership at all levels. These elements cannot be programmed. They can only develop in a decentralized environment that encourages individual initiative, trial and error and risk taking.

An extraordinary intensification of creativity is characteristic of our era. It appears naturally in the world of science and technology, but its economic implementation depends on the dynamism, commitment and decisions of entrepreneurs. It is important to bear this in mind when working out a model for sustainable development.

The concept of progress

Derailment of modernity

If one wishes to give meaning and purpose to the actions of firms one must think about the concept of progress and about the limits of material progress without purpose.

We have already seen that the rule of the 'single thought' and the dominance of an instrumental logic are in danger of isolating the economy and technology from the other dimensions of human progress. We have also seen that deviations in the market economy, particularly financial deviations, can have effects that go against the desired course of development. The ambiguities of technological acceleration, globalization and competitive games have been emphasized.

One of the most pertinent analyses of deviations in economic and technical systems is that by the French sociologist Alain Touraine (1992). I shall draw on this for my discussion.

The concept of progress was born with modernity. By freeing mankind from religious, political and cultural constraints the Renaissance, humanism and the Reformation gave birth to 'reason' and 'conscience', 'the subject' as two opposing but complementary forces.

The world of reason is governed by the natural laws that intelligence discovers and to which it is subject. Reason is what drives science and its applications – technology and production. It presides over the organization of society regulated by the law; it strives to replace arbitrariness and violence with law and the market.

The world of the subject arises from conscience, emotion and free will; it is 'the person's effort to make himself into an individual who is not subject to an instrumental logic' (ibid.); it is the anxious consciousness of the self, the questioning of meaning, the call for personal freedom and responsibility; it is the world of the emotional – the heart, the soul, love, religion and recognition of the other as a subject; it is also the world of doubt and questioning.

There are two internal lights that are more or less balanced: that of knowledge and that of emotion, 'two forces whose stormy relationships have drafted the history of modernity' (ibid.) Touraine's thesis is that modernity began as a liberation, but by breaking the balance between these two forces it has progressively been transformed into an instrument of domination and alienation.

In the fifteenth century modernity was experienced as an emancipation from medieval constraints. Optimism reigned: critical reason and scientific research would build a better world; government would become one of the 'fine arts'; the law and the state of law would free the people and encourage the entrenchment of civilized relations; freedom of individuals and trade would replace the oppression and planned economy of the states. The world might be ruled by a reason still enlightened by religious conscience, and the future promised to be better than the past.

The Renaissance and the Reformation were moments of miraculous equilibrium: 'Brunelleschi created the dome of Florence, a triumph of reason and calculation; Luther pushed man to become personally responsible by meditating on evil, human fragility and the necessity of salvation' (ibid.) The rational world of 'things' had not yet suffocated the world of people and the search for meaning. At that time the idea of progress related to human progress.

This equilibrium did not last. From the Enlightenment, there was a progressive dissociation of reason from the subject. Reason was gradually transformed into rationalism and became instrumental. The subject began to be hived off by concepts such as the social contract, or those proposed by Hobbes. The individual was returned to being a citizen (the French Revolution) or a consumer (contemporary capitalism).

A growing gap appeared between the objective world created by reason and the subjective world of conscience, between the 'warm' world of human beings and the 'cold' world of objects manipulated by techniques. The danger increased of a complete dissociation of the system from the players, the instruments from the meaning, the means from the ends and the economy from culture. Reason became an autonomous reality that increasingly imposed itself on the subject, 'a purely external power that... uses the resources of the ego (the subject) in order to build itself, but which possesses its own dynamic and develops itself under the pressure of a purely internal demand. The ego (the subject) is compelled to recognize this demand as a prompting force that uncompromisingly imposes on it its own constraints ... an anonymous process of self-establishment of reason' (Ladrière, 2001), and man was no more than the medium in this process.

I have already discussed the growing autonomy of the economy and technology in comparison with politics and ethics. In this regard, today we are witnessing a serious instrumental deviation: the market economy, propelled by technoscience, is becoming its own end. The system is dominating the players (Crozier and Friedberg, 1977) and locking itself into its own particular logic. It no longer has any other purpose than its own development.

In a manner relevant for our era, Touraine (1992) shows the terrible historical reactions of subjects in search of meaning against a society that no longer offers them anything. No longer fully finding a place in a world without purpose, individuals may fall victim to the great common myths that give them the illusion of rediscovering the society of human beings, the society of belonging, relationships with one another and a collectively experienced purpose. This was the case with national socialism and communism in the twentieth century. Today, and quite differently, this can be true of sects, fundamentalism and introverted identities.

Some people wonder whether it is still possible to speak of progress after a century of madness, bloodshed and extermination. Can we speak of the world and of history as though Auschwitz never existed (Gheshé, 1993)? Thereafter man was under no illusions about the wild animal that sleeps within him (Grousset, 1946).

Loss of balance between the world of reason and that of conscience can lead either to the development of a dominant system in an ethical and political vacuum, or to despair and disgust.

This type of reflection on progress leads us to question a development model that takes means for ends and reduces the progress of humanity to that of economics, science and technology.

Here comes again the age-old temptation of Prometheus to believe that material progress alone will cure mortals of the pangs of death. Must he be bound or should his vast creativity be let loose to find its purpose? Is it not time to restore to progress its ethical and political dimension?

Ambiguity revisited

Is economic and technical progress compatible with human progress, or are its autonomy and dynamism allowing it to elude social and political control to the point of completely imposing on us its technical and materialistic view of the future? Has it become its own end, with no regard for those who are excluded from it, or for the threats that weigh on our future?

In a globalizing society, is our development model still compatible with a better future, a more just society that is freer and more united, and with what philosophers call 'the good life'? This is the level at which the purpose of the firm must be questioned.

What do philosophers have to say on the matter? They view the problems from a higher level than do sociologists or economists, but they arrive at the same conclusions. They speak of limits, contradictions and threats, of power and responsibility, of questioning. They express the necessity of aiming our actions at human progress and basing our economic and technical choices on more universal values.

In an analysis of what contemporary humanism might be, the philosopher Jean Ladrière (2001) is prudently optimistic and opens up certain perspectives. For him, today's world is characterized both by an intensification of human creativity and by the presence of limits and contradictions. These two elements come close to the theme of this book and lead us to consider the meaning of human actions.

The intensification of creativity

For Ladrière four domains are especially representative of modern creativity: science, technology, politics and art. The first two relate directly to our argument.

In the domain of science, 'the search for knowledge is no longer the simple recording of what happens in an external world, independently of any initiative, it is an active intervention in the cosmic processes, guided by suggestions of abstract structures from the mathematical universe. Truth is not given, it is constructed' (ibid.).

In the domain of technology,

> starting from a certain critical threshold, technological innovations are no longer responses to a prior demand, but precede demand and create it. Innovation itself is made possible by scientific

progress and is increasingly organized according to trial and error and following the same form of collective and systematized research as science. Modern technology replaces the natural world in which man participates with a world built of artefacts, in which man becomes the operator of a demiurgy that he creates himself, but which more and more narrowly controls his own activities. (Ibid.)

This type of creativity raises questions about its own purpose. It requires a search for meaning:

What is at stake in the construction of the new science of nature is not only the content of the theoretical principles implemented, but the very idea of science. What is at stake in technological invention is not only the solution of particular practical problems, but the very possibility of the establishment of a technological world...The transforming action operates...from the awareness it has of its own power, recognized in the very works it produces... It must discover the objective possibilities they reveal and decide itself in this new reality it has created...This means that...historic creativity is basically the emergence of a responsibility that does not bear on particular decisions, but that concerns the historical condition of man as such. (Ibid.)

In other words the current intensification of creativity raises questions about the purpose of actions and directly questions every firm that would claim to be responsible.

The experience of limits, contradictions and ambiguities

The twentieth century struck a fatal blow on optimism. It highlighted the ambiguity of historical experience and the duality of mankind (reason and conscience). It has reminded us of the necessity of returning politics and ethics to the centre of our choices and strategies if we are to control the limits and contradictions of human activity:

The century that has just passed was largely marked by terrible collective ordeals, and as a result it was a time of disillusionment. We have witnessed the sombre and tragic side of history that Shakespeare forcefully described as 'full of noise and fury'. The idea of the rule of reason has become, to say the least, highly problematic.

What has to be recognized is that, in our understanding of the project of reason, we have to take account of internal and external limitations, and also of the presence in history of a principle of adversity and the reality of evil. (Ladrière, 2001)

Ladrière lists the limitations imposed by the environment: those on living space, natural resources, drinking water, oxygen, demographic pressure and so on. He reminds us that we are now in a closed system and that scarcity has become a fundamental parameter.

Our system also has internal limitations, linked to complexity and the methods we use:

We know that, at least from a certain level of development, a completely centralized economic system loses its effectiveness. In more general terms, one might say that the extension of rational methods generates more and more complex systems that cannot be managed by traditional methods and that call for the invention of new, more formal tools. (Ibid.)

As for contradictions, Ladrière makes reference to the systemic deviations discussed in Part I of this book:

indirect effects that are produced by the action itself without being expressly desired and that are even the exact opposite of what was wanted. This is the kind of phenomenon that we see in the functioning of the economy, and also in technological development. The ecological crisis consists of phenomena of this type. (Ibid.)

When discussing the ambiguity of progress and the bad use to which it can be put, he refers to the voluntary threats to man himself:

There is a sort of contradiction that is directly and deliberately created by human action and that...bears on man himself, and affects his integrity and dignity. We must recognize the presence of a principle that remains outside the domain of rationality and defies any purely rational explanation. It is something that has long been recognized in philosophical thought and is what Kant calls radical evil. (Ibid.)

This does not lead to abandonment of the idea of true human progress but to a requirement to fit our creativity into ethical and political processes worthy of the name. Ladrière proposes two basic paths. The first is to:

> introduce the questions into the democratic debate. The events in the latter part of the [twentieth] century have taught us that what might be called political pathology is not a fatality, and that democracy, at least as an inspiring idea, remains a powerfully active force that is perhaps even more effective than ever. (Ibid.)

It is by developing its political culture that the firm will be able to extend its aims and better position its actions to serve the common good and the general interest. We shall discuss this in the next chapter.

The other path is that of ethics. In a globalizing economy we can no longer define the purpose of the firm and the market economy without reference to a sufficiently universal system of values. The universal declaration of human rights (United Nations, 1948) was a first step along this path.

The *raison d'être* of the firm

Setting out the aims and purpose of economic and technical progress involves fitting this progress into the greater totality of human progress.

Economics is only part of the whole and it cannot dominate human society by imposing its restricted vision of progress. Other forms of progress exist in the domains of culture, society, politics, spirituality, education and so on. While economic progress may encourage some of them, it does not cover the whole field of human progress. We have also seen that deviations of the current system can cause regression and lead to negative or even destructive situations.

We must cease to claim that there is a quasi-automatic convergence between economic creativity and the global development of humanity. We must cease to assert that the economy and personal interests dictate our behaviour, and that to respond to global challenges we have only to place our faith in technical ingenuity and market indications.

The firm will only become responsible if it subscribes to an all-embracing view of human progress and sustainable development. To establish the purpose of the firm and the market economy it is necessary to answer the following questions. Economic and technical progress for what? For whom? How? These questions are of an ethical and political nature so the market is incapable of answering them on its own.

For what? Is it really necessary for our power of economic action and creative capacity to devote so much effort and so many resources to expanding markets and catering to a consumer society that is constantly excited and encouraged by feverish, invasive and often vulgar advertising? Are there no unsatisfied priority needs whose importance surpasses by far the pursuit of hyper-comfort or later Byzantine leisure?

For whom? Is it morally and politically acceptable to tolerate the exclusion of half the world's population from the benefits of a creative and dynamic economy that functions without it or against it? Are we going to continue to tolerate the paradoxical coexistence of historically unparalleled wealth and widespread poverty that affects several billion people?

How? Will the race for growth in which the rich countries are participating become increasingly independent of the problems of the planet? Will they continue to pollute the atmosphere, destroy the planet's limited resources and encourage a society that is individualistic, egoistic and enclosed in the bubble of its success and privileges?

It might be said that I am moving away from economic logic, but that is exactly my argument. We are concerned here with the political and moral questions that are being posed to the market economy and the firms that operate in it. The latter will only become responsible if they accept and integrate the answers to these questions into their aims and values.

Firms cannot respond to these questions by themselves. This is why they are increasingly drawn into political debate and ethical reflection. This constitutes a considerable change in culture that goes further than the majority of pronouncements on social responsibility.

From this viewpoint, the choice of aims and purpose stems more from a process than from a theoretical definition. It is based on a progressive collective awareness of our power of action and its necessary orientation towards the type of society we wish to build: which development model, which form of social justice, which type of education, which standard of health care and so on.

Neither the market nor shareholders alone are capable of driving forward this process. Broad consultation is necessary. Firms have much to bring to and learn from such consultations, provided they participate in an open and constructive way, as some business leaders have begun to do.

Firms will only be able to make a positive contribution if they adopt an ethics for the future and engage in public debate. They will have to question the appropriateness of an economic system that is considered good only because it is efficient. All this will lead them to broaden their aims and purpose and correct their strategies and practices, which to date have been confined to their own ambit.

What is required is a fundamental cultural transformation to provide the foundation of true responsibility. Economic performance will not be sufficient to make the firm legitimate if it does not rise to the new ethical, social and environmental challenges (Ellington, 1997).

It is not difficult to see that, with this approach, profit and shareholder value do not provide the appropriate *raison d'être*. They can be good instruments for measuring and conditioning development but they are means, not ends. Today these concepts are too narrow and too restricted to legitimate the firm.

Can one define the purpose of the firm without subscribing to a rigid framework that would become a new single thought? For each firm, purpose can only be defined by its activities, strategies and the ethical and political problems it encounters. We can only suggest a general orientation for the debate that has been necessitated by the acceleration of our creativity and recognitions of our limitations.

In a global economy the *raison d'être* of the firm is to ensure economic and technical progress that furthers human progress and facilitates the type of society we wish to have.

The concept that comes closest to this is sustainable development, provided the firm does not treat this as merely an instrument of public relations. It is not a question of conducting a defensive campaign or promoting a new image of legitimacy. It is by adopting a proactive stance that the firm will become responsible and position its actions in a wider context. New criteria will influence its strategic choices: the protection of the planet, respect for populations, greater social justice, prudence in the application of science.

The direction taken by development will not depend exclusively on the pressure of technologies, the financial markets or consumers stirred up by advertising, but on a true debate by society. Refusal to give an ethical and political meaning to the development model would accentuate its flaws and further diminish its legitimacy in a threatened world.

Prometheus was bound because he made material progress an end in itself. The pursuit of 'this infinite path open to men' would ensure their happiness and 'cure mortals of the pangs of death'. We now know this to be a lie: technical progress has not removed the anguish of death. The paths opened up by inventions and material progress can lead to chaos if attention is not paid to purpose, if it is made an end rather than a means. In the end Prometheus recognized that his approach did not provide the ultimate answer to mankind's problems: 'above art, above cunning and intelligence, destiny commands'. But when the chorus reproached him for his pride and urged him to control himself and submit to a moral order, he stood firm: 'May lightning strike me with its flame, may thunder roar from the bowels of the earth and may Zeus unleash the bound forces, overturn the world and reduce it to chaos, nothing will weaken me.' To which the chorus replied: 'You have not learned wisdom, Prometheus, your heart hardens; the pride of the mad is a weak force.' Excess, hubris, madness.

Prometheus's words were answered by the loud voice of Moses, announcing calamities that were close to our current preoccupations. Speaking of the development of the Promised Land, he said:

> If thou wilt not hearken unto the voice of the Lord thy God [if you do not give an ethical dimension to development]...cursed thou shalt be in the city, and cursed thou shalt be in the field. Cursed shall be thy basket and thy store. Cursed shall be the fruit of thy body, and the fruit of thy land, the increase of thy kine, and the flocks of thy sheep.
>
> The Lord shall send upon thee cursing, vexation, and rebuke, in all that thou settest thine hand unto for to do, until thou be destroyed and until thou perish quickly...until he have consumed thee from off the land, whither thou goest to possess it.

And thy heaven that is over thy head shall be brass, and the earth that is under thee shall be iron...

The Lord shall cause thee to be smitten before thine enemies...

The Lord shall smite thee with madness, and blindness, and astonishment of heart. (Deuteronomy: 28, 15–28)

7
The Ethics of the Future

Who is my neighbour?

(Luke: 4.10.29)

By wishing to be responsible, the firm is engaging in an ethical approach. Those which say they are responsible will respond through their actions to a system of values that outlines a concept of man, society and the future. If the firm wishes to lend meaning to its actions, if it wants to give a purpose to economic progress by fitting it to human progress, ethics are essential to enlighten choice and guide behaviour. We once again pose the question of whether one can conform to ethics while participating in a system that has none.

Do ethics come down to integrity? We know that the market economy and capitalism are based on trust and respect for the rules of the game. If these disappear the system disintegrates. Here it is a question of integrity that ensures respect for norms: truth, openness, honesty and so on. But these are not enough. We must also know what type of world we want to build together.

Located in the march of time, men are historical beings and their actions build the world. They are responsible for the future and for the society they create. This responsibility becomes all the greater as their creativity and powers grow. As we have seen, this is the case with the firm and the economic and technical systems it drives.

To refuse to integrate ethics into the functioning of the firm on the pretext that the economy has its own logic amounts to locking oneself into an instrumental approach (the single thought) and depriving the firm of its social legitimacy. If they are led by a logic of

116

means rather than of *ends*, some honest managers risk belonging to the category of people so well described by Péguy: 'the world is full of honest people, who can be recognized by the clumsiness with which they make their dishonesties' (Péguy, 1917).

If ethics are an interrogation on the type of world we want to build together, in a democratic society they must be the subject of a wide-ranging, open and continuous debate. The responsible firm will actively participate as its strategies will affect the future of the world. Many long-term decisions are being taken 'in the dark', such is the rapid advancement of science and the difficulty of predicting the consequences of its discoveries.

In an uncertain, pluralist and complex world, one can no longer rely entirely on established norms or codes of conduct pronounced from on high. That is why it is necessary to open up places in the firm and in the society where this ethical dimension and the concrete responsibilities that flow from it can be called forth. It involves a permanent attitude of collective interrogation. It will stem from a collective process rather than from an imposed code of conduct prepared in advance and quickly set in stone. It involves developing in the firm a culture that will progressively increase the awareness of the unsustainability of our development model and an evolution of our behaviour.

Finally, in the face of the current political vacuum, globalization and the rapid development of science and technology, ethics offer the most effective weapon against the single thought. When laws do not exist or are inadequate, ethics among the players are essential to bring about changes and correct the deviations of a system deprived of a clear purpose.

Ethics of conviction

Ethics are our values, our moral convictions that govern the difference between what we perceive as good and what we perceive as evil, or more subtly, between better and worse. They stem from the conscience and guide our choices and behaviour. In a globalizing world, deciding what type of society we wish to build should be based on values that are as universal as possible.

Is this realistic in a world torn between galloping modernity, the single thought and individualism on the one hand, and tradition, rejection of modern development and fundamentalism on the other?

Is it even possible in a pluralist western society that has distanced itself from religious belief and wishes to free itself from past constraints and present restrictions on creativity and personal expression, even if the latter lacks content or meaning?

Is it possible when we are committed to a 'utopia of the immediate' (Steiner, 1973) and the rejection of classic values? Are we not tempted to do away with all values and to bring about absolute freedom and total respect for the freedom of others? Some comments made at the time of the death of the philosopher Rawls address this clearly.

For example, 'Between a fundamentalist household and a homosexual couple wishing to adopt a child, there is no possible understanding of the concepts of good and evil. What must take priority is mutual respect for their freedom.' Or, 'One cannot agree on the good, let us therefore agree on the just, which is located beyond ethical choices that should only arise from private life; let us restrict ourselves to establishing rules that allow people to agree to live and work together for the best.'

If we pushed this reasoning too far, would we not risk putting everything on the same footing and causing the disappearance of criteria for good and evil, better and worse, and thus losing all sense of priorities? Would it then be possible to conceive of a desirable future and to build a more humane, united and peaceful world (Van Parijs, 1991)?

Would it not be dangerous to reduce everything to the rules of the game by abandoning the concept of value in a world where laws would not be able to regulate everything and where scientific, technological, economic and financial powers would rule with force and dynamism? As Václav Havel (1989) said, 'should we not have the courage to forge an order of values for ourselves?'

In the view of Pope John-Paul II, 'Believing in the possibility of knowing a universally valid truth is not at all a source of intolerance. On the contrary, it is the necessary condition for a sincere and authentic dialogue between people' (Papal Encyclical, 1998).

This book is not the place for a profound discussion of values or their universal purpose. Rather I simply wish to highlight the necessity of possessing a moral imperative to guide our choices and behaviour.

As Kant (2004) put it: 'Act in such a way that you might also wish that the rule guiding your action would become a universal law.'

This imperative found its first concrete manifestation in the Universal Declaration of Human Rights (United Nations, 1948).

> Its proclamation is certainly an historic event of prime importance that gives concrete expression, if only partial, to the humanism of our time beginning to emerge. But this expression must be considered as only an approximation of an inspiring vision in which we can detect the manifestation of the ethical dimension of man...
>
> The idea of human rights concerns the human being as such, in his individuality and in the characteristics of his culture, beliefs and convictions, but from a point of view that is universal...
>
> It is by virtue of this universal quality of being the bearer of rights that the individual is recognized in his uniqueness. Here we find the definition of a view in which universality does not function like a principle of totality, but as being in itself the recognition and guarantee of differences. (Ladrière, 2001)

In his interesting essay on this topic, Jean-Claude Guillebaud (2001) suggests returning to a categorical imperative and proposes, the principle of humanity as the basis of contemporary ethics.

He discusses the current deviations of the triple revolution – genetics, economics and information technology – and warns of the slow and insidious destruction of man's integrity, conscience and environment. He refers to the Nuremberg medical code (1946–47) 'which, for the first time, proposed to set rules and limits on all experimentation on mankind.... It reformulated an imprescriptible principle: every man, woman and child – even mentally handicapped, even without conscience, even without language, even dying – is separately and fully a member of the human race. As such, he/she is the holder of a dignity that nothing or nobody may violate. This is how the requirement for human dignity was revalued at a higher level. We still live with this requirement. Who would allow it to be contested?' (ibid.).

This is what Hans Jonas (2000) calls 'the sacrosanct character of the subject'. Recall that Jesus Christ based his religion on the principles of love and respect for one's neighbour (Matthew: 22: 37–40).

The moral imperative is the very basis of ethical behaviour. It imposes itself on us for itself and not for instrumental reasons of utility or performance. It disputes the validity of the cynicism portrayed by Bernis (1980): 'one rarely has the virtues that interest does not command', or the utilitarianism of some management gurus who claim that 'ethics pay' and ought to contribute to the firm's profits. This is clearly the opposite of the ethical approach and again reveals the low level of the single thought.

If we are to build a better world, therefore, it is important to affirm our values and nurture the humanism and wisdom needed to guide, orient and master creativity and an economic system that currently lacks purpose. This offers a means of escaping imprisonment in a logic of means and of restoring our capacity to discern the difference between price and value.

Ethics of responsibility

Ethics are not restricted to convictions or values. They also concern our actions and their consequences. Ethics are incarnated in action, and in this sense they constitute a commitment. This is where they become concrete.

Enlightened by convictions and values, the ethic of responsibility takes into account not only behaviour itself but also the consequences of decisions and actions. Intentions are not sufficient – responsibility must be taken for the consequences. The popular saying 'hell is paved with good intentions' clearly reflects the ethical inadequacy of an action or failure to act when responsibility for the consequences is not assumed.

'Ethics begins at the first cry of human suffering' (Feuerbach, 2001), at the moment when one confronts others (Levinas, 1972). It prevents us from being indifferent to others' suffering, especially if it is we who have caused it (see Fourez, 1988).

Max Weber put great emphasis on the necessity of complementing conviction with responsibility. More recently Paul Smets (2002) has reiterated the necessity of connecting these two dimensions. If an action is not guided by convictions and values it has no ethical character.

For the firm, the first application that comes to mind is that of integrity. It is often here that ethical reflection by business people stops: being successful and profitable without lying, stealing, cheating or unduly harming others. Respect for the law and the rules of the game is obviously very important since our economic system is based on trust and good faith. In developed countries these minimum requirements are closely monitored and punishment may be meted out in the case of serious failings.

Nothing is perfect in human affairs, but the majority of executives and managers are honest at the personal level, even if sometimes 'accommodations are made with heaven' and if, 'according to various needs, it is a science to stretch the bonds of our conscience and to correct the badness of our action with the purity of our intention' (Molière).

But is honesty sufficient on its own? Beyond personal honesty, is it not necessary to extend the responsibility of the economic players to the model itself, and to investigate its negative aspects and the consequences of its deviations? If the imperatives are the dignity of mankind and the survival of the planet, must not managers take more responsibility for the functioning of the system they drive and its effect on those whom it alienates, excludes, dismisses or renders outdated, and for those whose traditional structures are destroyed if they are less efficient or dynamic?

If ethics begin at the first cry of human suffering, is it not necessary to pay attention to the cries of those who suffer in one way or another as a result of our development model, instrumental logic and single thought, to listen to them directly when possible, or to their spokespersons? The latter often act as the conscience for the mistakes and dangers that our development model spreads around the world. NGOs in particular fulfil this function. They highlight suffering, warn of possible catastrophes, create a sense of urgency and denounce our collective indifference, egoism and lack of values. Even if their voices are sometimes strident and their claims exaggerated, they are often bearers of morality.

The ethic of responsibility consists in encouraging this type of action and 'siding with the people' by changing our methods of development in order to promote greater humanity and solidarity. If the firm wants to become responsible, it must concern itself with these matters and stop believing that they are the subject only of public action.

Of course the firm cannot deal with everything, but with its resources and creativity it can help to transform the system it drives and to reduce the negative consequences of its operation. 'It is true that we do not have to respond to all the misery in the world, the wars, hunger and injustice. However our ethics will remain an illusion if they do not refer us back to concrete situations, that is, if, in reflecting on specific domains of activity, we do not question the manner in which these domains are likely to be called forth by human distress' (Maesschalk, 1995).

During an ethics course at a business school an Enron executive was asked what he would do if he learned that one of his firm's products had the potential to cause harm. He is reported to have answered: 'I would continue to produce and sell it. My job as a businessman is to be a profit centre and to maximize shareholder income. It is up to the government to intervene if a product is dangerous' (Fusaro and Miller, 2002; see also *Financial Times*, 18 September 2002).

Perhaps a first step towards a true ethical attitude would be to reject indifference to anything that does not relate to the instrumental logic and listen to the cries of those who suffer because of our economic system. Indifference makes one deaf and blind. It is a rejection of humanity.

'We have played the flute and you have not danced. We have sung laments of mourning and you have not wept' (Luke 3.7.32). 'He saw him and passed on his way' (ibid., 4.10.31).

Another step would be to engage with entities such as public authorities, unions, NGOs and so on in order to examine the possibility of a better oriented development model.

Ethics for the future

We must go further still and take responsibility for the future. According to Bergson (1932), conscience is a thread between what has been and what will be, a bridge between the past and the future.

We have already seen that the traditional ethics based on proximity and simultaneity were insufficient because they were restricted to the presence of neighbours and the immediate consequences of actions. Science, technology and globalization have posed totally new questions and forced us look beyond this narrow framework.

Who is our neighbour today? Is it a passer-by, someone we meet casually or someone we know personally? Or is it a person that our economic actions can exclude, alienate or destroy; a person whose very existence is threatened by a system that pollutes the planet and promotes an unprecedented acceleration of technoscience with no clear purpose.

Is it not necessary to broaden our responsibilities and ethical concerns to include a collective suffering that is being made unbearable by the deviations and excesses of our development model?

The consequences of firms' decisions and strategies are often difficult to predict. Scientific, technical and financial choices bear upon an increasingly distant future and their outcomes are rarely known with precision. Economic and technical evolution is more rapid than ethical, political or legal reflection. The *Homo faber* is beginning to dominate the *Homo sapiens*.

To this is added the complexity of our management systems, understanding of which is beginning to elude us. There is a danger of the contradictions mentioned by Ladrière (2001) and the possibility of undesirable indirect effects, or even results that are opposite to those expected.

A major example is research and its commercial applications. Having become important weapons in the competitive arsenal, science and technology are caught up in the market logic, which accelerates their progress and uses them immediately without asking sufficient questions about their impact on society or the environment. A typical attitude is: one presses on, one ensures market share, and any negative effects can be corrected later.

Who can predict all the consequences of the unfettered distribution of genetically modified organisms, the genetic manipulation of living beings, global warming and accelerated globalization of the market economy? As Valéry (1988) said, 'man quite often knows what he does, he never knows what is done by what he does'.

Since firms are the major players in a system that continues to spread and to increase in complexity, are they not responsible for reflecting on the new ethical stakes they are helping to create and on the new orientations of our development model?

History is irreversible and the future world will be what we ourselves construct (Fourez, 1988; Gesché, 1993). This threatened and suffering world, 'traversed by evil' is still evolving and we are responsible for its development and humanization. This is where a set of ethics for the future will find its full meaning.

The philosopher Hans Jonas (2000) offers very enlightening reflections on this subject. He maintains that the new dimensions of human action and 'the monstrous progress of technology' and its power over man call for an ethic of forecasting and for a sense of responsibility of a sufficient degree to match these challenges. He refers to the 'sacrosanct character' of man and warns against scientific and technical orientations that might undermine it: 'Never must the existence or essence of man in his entirety be called into question in the gamble of action... Concerning the life of humanity, the principle stands (which is not necessarily always valid for the individual patient) that even imperfect medicines must be preferred to the highly promising drastic remedy that carries the risk of the patient's death.' Therefore no risk that might damage humanity!

Jonas adds to this the protection of the planet as a condition for humanity's survival. Human actions with no clear purpose are threatening biological diversity and the necessary conditions for life on earth. These stakes are sufficient to justify extending the ethical investigation beyond mere relationships between people.

The new categorical imperative can be formulated in the following way: act in such a way that the effects of your action are compatible with permanent life on Earth; or to put it negatively, act in such a way that the effects of your action do not destroy the possibility of a good life in the future. Or simply, do not compromise the conditions required for the indefinite survival of humanity.

Jonas proposes some principles to give substance to this approach.

One of the elements of the ethics for the future is *to anticipate more* and to gain an idea of the distant effects of our decisions. The past may not necessarily enlighten the future. 'What we have to fear has not yet been precisely experienced and may have no resemblance to current or past experience' (ibid.). This representation of the future 'will not impose itself automatically but must be procured deliberately. Obtaining this representation through thought about the future is the preliminary requirement of this ethics' (ibid.). Jonas proposes the setting up of a science for hypothetical prediction, a 'comparative futurology'. This will require us to move away from short-term thinking and to turn our eyes towards distant and unfamiliar horizons. This is all the more important in that the future is represented by no one, and has no spokesperson or authorized defender.

Another element is what Jonas calls the heuristics of fear:

> This is only the vision of a distortion of man that produces the
> concept of *man that has to be protected* and we need the threat
> against man's image – and quite specific types of threat – in order to
> assure ourselves of a *true image of man* thanks to the fear emanating
> from this threat... We only know what is at stake when we know
> that it is at stake. (Ibid.)

Here there is a *requirement for concern* about any decision that affects
the future in a fundamental way.

Jonas also insists on the necessity to 'watch over beginnings'. He
fears that the cumulative dynamic of technological developments
will result in an uncontrolled spiral:

> Experience has shown that the developments set in motion by tech-
> nological action in order to achieve short-term goals have a tendency
> to become autonomous, that is, to acquire their own internal
> dynamic, an autonomous development as result of which they are not
> only irreversible but self-propelled forward and go beyond the short
> term desires and plans of those who act... Whereas the first step arises
> from our liberty, we are slaves to the second and all that follow. (Ibid.)

Added to the fact that the pace of technological development leaves
little time for corrections to be made, such corrections are becoming
increasingly difficult and the freedom to make them is diminishing.
This imposes on us a *principle of precaution* when making fundamental
choices, as well as a duty to stop any project that reveals itself to be
dangerous. Climate change is one domain in which this principle
should be applied systematically. Circumspection is at the heart of
ethical action.

Another principle is the following: the making of economic and
technical progress does not justify the possible risks when it involves
improving something that is already satisfactory. These risks 'are
not taken with the aim of saving what exists or abolishing what is
intolerable, but with the aim of continually improving what has
already been achieved, in other words, in the name of a progress
that, in the most ambitious case, aims to produce a paradise on
earth' (ibid.). This is a rational meliorism of a modern type.

Progress that is too risky is therefore placed 'under the heading of arrogance rather than under that of necessity, and the renunciation in the things that it allows... concern only the superfluous in comparison to the necessary' (ibid.). This is not acceptable when the consequences may be intolerable. There is therefore a *principle of selection*, meaning that not all progress is for the good.

This principle has been around for a long time, but the acceleration of the technosciences has tended to make us forget it. As Cicero put it, 'For honest people, is everything that can be done, to be done?' Sorting between the possibilities (Beck and Giddens, 1994) must be a priority if we are to build a proper future and commit ourselves to sustainable development.

The sacred character of mankind, the necessity to protect the planet, awareness, concern, prudence and selection – these are some of the basic principles and attitudes needed to underpin the ethics of the future and the responsibilities of the firm. They cannot be reduced to the adoption of a few new practices with a view to maintaining or increasing profits (Pruzan, 2003a; see also Pruzan, 2003b). It is for firms and management schools to transform them into concrete strategies and management theories.

An ethical culture in the firm

In a complex world, ethics are never simple. They can rarely be reduced to black and white facts of good or evil. They usually present themselves in terms of better or worse, light grey or dark grey. They may not be reduced to a code of conduct promulgated by management and faithfully applied by employees acting in conformity.

This is not what happens in organizations, especially when attitudes and convictions are involved. Excellent ethical codes existed in firms such as Enron and WorldCom but they did not prevent cheating, lying and misappropriations, or the establishment of a climate of immorality, greed and corruption.

In this domain we must go beyond the superficial practices and artificial image of honesty created for public relations reasons. We must go beyond a cosmetic approach and ask ourselves the following question: 'Are we truly advancing towards a doctrine for the twenty-first century or are we awarding ourselves with impunity a certificate of good conscience?' (Smets, 2003).

The firm must change its entire culture if it wants to become responsible and transform its behaviour. This is why movements of Corporate Social Responsibilities (CSR) will only really improve our model of development if they agree to base their approach on solid concepts and values going beyond the stage of tools, instruments or exchange of good practices.

In the ethical domain, cultural evolution consists of developing ethics as basic thoughts that permeate all levels of the firm and each of its departments: finance, marketing, research and so on. If the firm wants to behave in a responsible way, retain its autonomy and the freedom required for creativity, and if it wants to avoid having the law regulate everything, it must make ethics an integral part of its culture, strategies and operations.

The content of the ethics adopted will obviously depend on the sector of activity, the size of the firm and the countries in which it operates. Moreover they will evolve in line with new problems posed by technical progress, growing complexity and the globalization of the economy. That is why not everything can be codified. In a decentralized economic system, ethics depend more on the conscience of the players and the values that guide them than on a list of prescribed topics.

The development of a new culture arises from permanent collective questioning. It involves a continuous search for responses to new problems that are often unusual and ambiguous and for which there is no pre-established response.

In order to do this the firm can create an ethical space in which the cultural process becomes visible, active, continuous and faces up to the 'inexhaustible complexity of the real' (Maesschalk, 1995). Such a space will be where new attitudes develop; a place of questioning, awakening, concern, listening; a place where the will to understand other views prevails over the will to condemn what is perceived as hostile or critical, such as comments by NGOs.

This will be a place where questioning is accepted, where ethical judgement is refined by facing up to what is desirable and what is possible, the greatest good and the least evil, values and realities. A place where 'the best [will] be distinguished from the worst, the extraordinary from the impossible' (Retz, 1956). A place where necessary compromises will be accepted and where we make prudent use of our power to respond to the challenges and contradictions that beset us. A place that will become activated, especially in 'ethical moments':

> one describes as ethical moments those situations in which the approach to adopt is anything but clearly defined because the ends are not clear, or perhaps are numerous and at least partially contradictory, when the relationships between the ends and the means are... far from being unequivocal, and when generalization is impossible since no concrete situation is completely identical to another. (Cobbaut, 1997)

At the level of the economic system as a whole, such places for ethical debate ought to be multiplied. Many professional associations, for example, are beginning to enter into such debates. As for interprofessional employers' associations, they do not yet really play this role. They ought to broaden their traditional mission, which chiefly involves defending the interests of their members and often forces them to adopt the lowest common denominator.

Other groups are being formed to promote the concept of sustainable development (for example the World Business Council for Sustainable Development) and social responsibilities. They could become the ethical spaces we are discussing. In Europe the associations of Christian managers and young employers have long served as ethical spaces. There are also many circles for reflection and study, business institutes and ethical groups where people can work out responses to the challenges of the future and deviations of the market economy. One of the best known of these is the European Business Ethics Network (EBEN). However it is questionable whether these efforts are sufficiently numerous and bold to allow a new model to evolve and replace the single thought with ethics worthy of the name.

Here convergence is needed: 'united action – protected from moralizing temptations – connected at several levels... international organizations, states, non-governmental organizations, families, teaching, justice, the media' (Smets, 2003).

The ethical culture of the firm is thus based on individual and collective awareness and on the integration of ethics into the attitudes and everyday behaviour of the players. The part played by managers is clearly important. If they are very demanding of themselves in matters of ethics they will expect this of the other members of the firm. If there is consistency between the values they hold and their behaviour, the adoption of an ethical organizational culture will be less difficult and more credible.

In organizations the attitude of top management often serves as the model. It sets the tone and operates in a more efficient way than formal rules. Speaking of the ideal philosopher, Seneca says 'he does not teach the truth, he is its witness'. Cicero adds that 'the state resembles the soul of its chiefs'. Ethical behaviour stems from this approach.

The basis of moral authority is what researchers in geopolitics call soft power. It consists of the values, moral consistency and atmosphere of confidence that reign in a firm. It is neither economic nor technical power or tools, but everything that reaches and convinces the heart and soul of people.

While the part played by top management is of vital importance, there will only be a true ethical culture if it is adopted by the whole workforce and everyone feels a sense of responsibility. Describing a long tradition of honesty, one American employer said 'everyone at Dupont knew where the line was that was not to be crossed; if he only saw that line, it meant that he was already too close to it; if he crossed it, he had to find employment elsewhere' (Kroll, 2002).

This case concerned only honesty – the responsible firm must go further. 'The reply to the unacceptable must be expressed and consolidated every day. Every time a Creon appears, an Antigone must be reborn. Everyone is responsible. One stone per person' (Smets, 2003).

Ethics and the technosciences

It is not the aim of this book to analyze the content or applications of ethics in the firm as there is already a considerable body of literature on the subject. I shall therefore restrict myself to the domain that is essential for my argument, namely that of the technosciences. It is science, which today is tightly bound to technology, that poses the most unusual questions in matters of ethics, beginning with its own status.

Science cannot be shielded from ethics

While the independence of science and its freedom of approach are the reasons for its excellence, the use of its results and the orientations of its research step into the realm of ethics (Lambert, 1999). There are several reasons for this.

The first is *the ambiguity of its applications*. Science has always been a source of optimism and wonder for mankind, but also of concerns and fears. The myth of Prometheus clearly alludes to this, as does the story of the tree of knowledge in the Bible. Sophocles (1967) also referred to this ambiguity: 'with his ingenious knowledge which exceeds all expectation man progresses towards evil or towards good'.

The second reason is its *proliferation and acceleration*, which are outstripping the understanding of people and the pace of social debate.

Steiner (1973) provides a good description of

the conviction, rooted in the heart of the Western personality, that investigation must go forward, that such momentum is in conformity with nature and meritorious in itself, that man is devoted to the pursuit of truth.... We open the gates to Bluebeard's castle in succession because 'they are there', because each leads to the next, according to the process of intensification by which the spirit defines itself... We pursue reality wherever it leads us...

The real problem is to know if one should persist with certain research, if society and the human spirit, at their stage of evolution, will be able to tolerate the truths to come. It is possible – and here there are already dilemmas such as history has never known – that the next door opens on realities unbearable for our mental equilibrium and for our meagre moral reserves...

Who will say if what awaits us constitutes a trap, if the link between speculative thought and the problems of survival that underpin our civilization is not in the process of breaking?... the 'positive truths' that the scientific laws conceal are transformed into a jail, darker than that of Piranese, a prison in which the future is locked. It is these 'facts' and not man that control the course of history...

I am waiting for us to push open the last gate of the castle, even if it opens, or perhaps because it opens, onto realities that are beyond the range of comprehension and the authority of man.

A third reason why science should be subject to ethics is its *increasingly close union with technology*. Firms have turned it into a competitive weapon. The time between research and concrete application is ever shorter and there is less and less public debate. It is economic and financial criteria that determine the transformation of scientific discoveries into commercial truths.

This confers on the technosciences an immense power to influence the evolution of human society. This influence is usually beneficial.

Materially, the leap forward is considerable and quite visible. These are the 'miracles' of technology, medicine and science. Human beings have, in much greater numbers than previously, the chance of reaching manhood, of having normal children, and of emerging from a thousand years of meagre existence. To neglect a truth so obvious and so full of hope is proof of a flagrant snobbery. Imagine a world without chloroform, suggested C. S. Lewis. (Ibid.)

But, at the same time it opens the door to apocalypses, such as nuclear wars or genetic manipulation, that may degrade humanity or destroy it. According to François Jacob, Nobel Prize winner for medicine, genetic manipulation

appears to border on the supernatural. It brings back from the darkness of time some of the myths rooted in the anguish of mankind. It causes the terror that conjures up in us the vision of monsters, the repugnance associated with the idea of hybrids, beings united against nature ... This [genetic knowledge] calls to mind evil knowledge, the epitome of forbidden knowledge ... It has become the subject of the greatest accusation made against science: giving biologists the power to demean and enslave the human body and spirit. (Jacob, 1997)

Seized on by an amoral or purposeless economic system and at liberty to impose their choices on us, the technosciences could enclose us in a world that would make Huxley's *Brave New World* look tame in comparison. 'The sciences bombard us with information about what we can do ... but it does not follow that it suits us to do it, still less that we should do everything that is made possible for us' (Moussé, 1989).

If we want science not to be subservient to commercial logic, we must make a distinction between fundamental research, the free pursuit of truth and its transformation into utility (Lambert, 1999).

The final reason for applying ethics to science lies in its *epistemological limits* (ibid.). Science is only one of the sources of knowledge available to us. It only provides us with that part of reality that it can discover through observation and experimentation. It says nothing about the uniqueness of people, nothing about meaning or purpose, nothing significant about moral suffering, evil or destiny. These vital matters lie outside its sphere, but they are at the heart of our political choices and the building of our future.

The gap between the technosciences and society

As soon as one looks at concrete examples one is struck by the growing gap between the technosciences and people. Caught up in a competitive and marketing dynamic, technoscience is increasingly in the hands of firms alone and its uses are often decided upon without prior debate, sometimes unwisely and often without ethical reflection. Firms seize new scientific discoveries and try to exploit them as quickly as possible in order to be the first on the world market.

As we have seen, this can be beneficial when there is no major stake for society. But when innovations call certain values into question it is necessary to control their application and remove them from the narrow confines of commercial logic. If monopolized by a single thought system, science could become scientism.

For a long time ethical and political controls, though weak, have been considered adequate. The bodies responsible for the control of drugs and foodstuff, such as the Food and Drug Administration in the US, are seen as protecting consumers. But can this still be claimed when we feed cows with animal by-products, want to patent and sell human embryos, and grow transgenic plants without completely knowing their effects on the environment? Such activities are arousing people's fear and they are beginning to lose confidence in what governments and firms tell them.

The case of genetically modified organisms is a good example of the current confusion. In response to pressure from some chemical firms the US government authorized the production and sale of certain transgenic crops. It then put political pressure on the EU and a number of other countries to open their frontiers to these products. Those countries that resisted were threatened with reprisal or accused of pursuing 'bad science'. The advantages of these products for poor countries were highlighted without revealing their disadvantages. Without objectivity or good faith, it was claimed that scientific knowledge about these crops was complete and that there was no danger to human health or the environment.

As a consequence millions of hectares were given over to genetically modified organisms (GMOs). In the US, they now account for 75 per cent of soya production, 71 per cent of cotton and 34 per cent of maize. World-wide, more than 20 per cent of crops are GMOs. The EU has resisted this development in the name of precaution, along with a number of other countries. In contrast to the US, the EU does not see GMOs as a commercial opportunity but as an issue involving health and the environment.

What do the scientists say? The most recent serious-minded research advocates prudence.[1] The findings are subtle but clear. As foodstuffs the current GMOs appear to be harmless and might offer nutritional benefits to poor countries. They might even improve health by reducing the use of pesticides, the presence of mycotoxins and soil pollution. But nothing can be said about the new or improved GMOs now being prepared by firms and that are not subject to strong controls or tests. As for the environment, while researchers tend to disagree, one thing is certain: GMOs are threatening other plants via cross-pollination. The seriousness of the consequences of this is not yet known and opinions differ widely in respect of the possible reduction in biodiversity. However the latest research has clearly shown that some GMOs are adversely affecting biodiversity. This is true of genetically modified beet and rape.

Do we now know enough to move onward, or should we continue the moratorium on GMOs long enough to allow us to increase our knowledge and refine our judgement?

In addition to the findings on biodiversity, recent research on GMOs has revealed several important things. For example it is scientifically possible to arrive at conclusive findings by working through case by case, plant by plant, as is already done for drugs. Also, it has been revealed that firms that produce GMOs do not conform to the principle of precaution and ought to be subject to greater supervision and control. It is interesting to note that it was pressure by society that caused governments to react – yet another example of the technosciences advancing faster than ethical political behaviour.

It is not the aim of this chapter to participate in the debate on GMOs but to highlight the necessity of a new ethical and political approach in the face of scientific breakthroughs.

The above discussion was to do with agriculture, but the same questions arise for the status of the embryo, cloning, climate change and so on. It is time to equip ourselves with structures for analysis and decision making that make more concrete use of ethics and apply the principle of precaution.

When the stakes are so high, the decision to go ahead cannot be left to firms whose criteria are chiefly commercial and financial, or to bodies of certification and control whose field of activity is restricted to certain sectors and whose knowledge develops less quickly than that of the firms in question.

As for the firms themselves, those that want to be seen as responsible must adopt a more ethical approach. The case of the 'terminator' seeds produced by Monsanto provides a good illustration. The crops grown from these seeds were infertile, which forced farmers to buy seed each year rather than save their own, which had been the normal practice in the past. Here we have the enslavement of the buyer by the producer, with all the pressures that brings. In the face of furious public opinion, Monsanto was forced to back down.

The same might happen on a much larger scale if the European Commission carries out its plan to test 30 000 chemical substances that might carry risks for health or the environment. The US is already accusing the EU of intending to use this to erect customs barriers. American and many European firms are protesting vociferously about the costs and constraints, which could undermine their competitiveness or even threaten their survival (*Financial Times*, 14 May 2003).

There we see two different approaches to economic development, and once again it will be necessary to find a balance between protecting entrepreneurial dynamism and adopting ethics for the future.

Science and the ethical debate

Given the acceleration of scientific advances and their growing variety and complexity, it is necessary to create in firms and society places for dialogue, in which people can not only debate the discoveries of science and technological breakthroughs, but also influence the use to which they are put and the conditions for their implementation. In this domain the ethical spaces discussed earlier would facilitate the search for concrete links between private decisions and the necessary public regulations. Participation in this dialogue should not be restricted to scientists. They are not the only people who are able to ask the right questions. They do not possess a monopoly on knowledge or human experience. 'The danger for the scientist, is not to measure the boundaries of his science and therefore of his knowledge. It is mixing what he believes with what he knows. Above all, it is the certainty of being right ... Scientists do not sufficiently rub up against the rest of society before proposing a doctrine whose application depends above all on that society' (Jacob, 1997).

As for the creators of technology, we should beware of their technical logic. They are often so dazzled by their new creations that they are blind or indifferent to the uses to which they might be put. A good example is the title given to an exhibition held in Washington in 2003, relating to the atomic bomb dropped on Hiroshima: 'A magnificent technological achievement'.

A dialogue between experts and those who are concerned about the significance and uses of new discoveries would help to avoid or limit their most negative applications: human cloning, eugenics, ever more destructive weapons and so on. It is important for society, social actors and users to participate in the debate, as well as representatives of various fields of human knowledge, such as philosophy, sociology, the law, religion and so on. Only a multidisciplinary approach can inform the building of the world to come.

A new methodology is required to lead this type of dialogue and guide the choices (see Lambert, 1999). It could be based on the following elements:

- Transparency and honesty: experts must divulge everything they know and admit to what they do not know; scientific journals should only publish findings whose rigour and independence can be proved.
- A thorough analysis of the potential applications of new scientific discoveries, their advantages, disadvantages, risks, conditions for implementation and so on.

- A search for alternatives if discoveries present serious risks; alternative products or technique to be proposed rapidly in the event of a major failure of new technologies or new products; but this is a major constraint and are there not already irreversible situations that risk enclosing us in a world that we would not have wished for?
- The monitoring of results over the years and regular updating of studies and previous enquiries.
- The will and power to halt new activities that might go wrong and become major risks.
- Permanent debate, for research is an unpredictable process: 'one can never know how it will evolve; it is therefore futile to hope to predict the direction that a science may follow' (Jacob, 1997).

This new and difficult domain should be made subject to systematic studies and rigorous ethical debate at the global level. In the absence of a more objective and better coordinated approach at the international level we risk locking ourselves into 'situations where one can do no more than make mistakes' (Retz, 1956).

8
Societal Debate and New Consultations

It is a serious act of folly to want to be wise by oneself.

(La Rochefoucauld)

Who wishes to speak now?

(Thucydides)

At the heart of politics lies the problem of power, its devolution, exercise and control. Power is at the centre of every organization and it is through power games that governments, firms, administrations, unions and NGOs are governed. One can understand nothing of how they function unless one is aware of the influences and methods of persuasion or constraint that drive and control them.

In our system economic and financial power belongs mainly to business executives and shareholders, who generally exercise it under the pressure of markets while respecting the law. They have the freedom to encourage dynamism, initiative and creativity in the model they drive.

In matters of strategy, finance, organization and so on, these leaders have the habit of deciding and acting without seeking much external consultation. They consider that they alone are responsible for the performance of their firm and its financial results.

Economics and technology are their domain. They wish to be allowed as much freedom as possible and to be trusted to decide on their strategic orientation: competition and the market will provide sufficient control to ensure productivity, initiative and progress. Labour unions' struggles and claims will translate part of this economic progress into social advancement. If firms' actions have negative external consequences the public powers are there to deal with them: 'leave the economic games to us, the state can look after the rest'. The first part of this book describes the instrumental rationality that tends to isolate economic and financial action from its social, cultural and political aspects.

Today the above concept of economic power is being called into question. The current trend towards broader debate and increased transparency calls for a new political culture in the firm.

When confronted with the deviations inherent in our development model and the dangers of poorly regulated globalization, the most enlightened business leaders agree to open up a debate on the directions of the economic system they operate and to take them into account in their long-term strategies. This is new. For two centuries any challenge to their power or any attempt to limit it were perceived as a threat to them.

Apart from a few exceptions, extracting measures for social progress from them was a hard-fought struggle. Even today, critical analyses of our development model, setting aside the virulent attacks by NGOs, are unacceptable and seem groundless to many businessmen. If we are to change this and see the first efforts of responsible firms imitated by a great number of enterprises, a cultural transformation is as necessary as in the field of ethics.

It is again a question of changing mentalities, attitudes and long-established practices. The whole climate of the firm must be changed if we are to escape the grip of the foolish views of Frederick Taylor (1965), architect of the scientific organization of work, who recommended 'replacing the government of men with the administration of things'.

If firms want to emerge from this narrow rationalism and rediscover their social dimension, they must develop a political culture in the full sense of the term; they must integrate their actions into public life and participate in debates on the common good and future directions. This would constitute a broadening of their purpose and facilitate the adoption of ethics for the future:

> Plutarch remarked that ancient philosophy was no more than the science of government. The seven sages, he said, with the exception of one, were only concerned with politics and morality and, although the Greeks were subsequently to pay attention to

the abstract sciences, we can see that their highest degree of esteem was for active philosophy, and their true cult was for the governors of the cities and their legislators. (Montesquieu)

Debate and questioning

Democracy is the form of political organization that is best suited to modern societies. Debate is its very condition and principal means. Jacqueline de Romilly (1992) reminds us that the adoption of democracy in Athens at the time of the Greek–Persian wars gave an unforeseen dimension to common debate.

The most innovative principle was

to invite thousands of citizens to a debate of words and ideas that was always open ... To speak, explain and convince one another: that was what Athens was proud of and what the texts never cease to extol ... So Euripides, when he celebrates democracy, through the mouth of Theseus in *The Suppliantes*, writes with panache: 'As for liberty, it is in these words: who wants, who can give some wise advice to his country? There, as he wishes, everyone can shine, or be silent. Can one imagine finer freedom? ... This 'who wishes to speak now?' seems to have haunted and amazed the Athenians. (Ibid.)

Today many citizens speak out. Their words on our economic system are often critical, sometimes virulent. NGOs have stepped up their attack on a development model that they view as unjust and dangerous, and condemn the poor control of globalization.

By denouncing the defects of a market economy that is left to its own devices, and stressing the urgent need for reform, protesters play their role of citizens to the full and fulfil a prophetic function, even if their analyses are sometimes inadequate or biased, their methods dubious and, in certain cases, unacceptable.

Some firms are beginning to listen to the words of protest, but the traditional culture of many others often prevents the opening up of true dialogue. A very important European employer said to me recently: 'Dialogue with the unions or governments we are used to and we regard as useful. As for the NGOs, they bring me out in spots: they are not legitimate, they are aggressive and they refuse any serious discussion.' It is a fact that the stand taken by some NGOs does not facilitate mutual discussion: superficial analyses, violent action, baseless or overgeneralized accusations and the rejection of dialogue, all discourage openness by employers. However it is also true that the employers' single thought and traditional culture have not encouraged communication or debate on the directions of the system or the purpose of the firm.

The most enlightened firms understand that a cultural evolution in political matters will occur through acceptance of open debate with those who question the development model. This type of debate would be democratic. If the firm wishes to integrate its economic actions into the wider canvas of ethics and politics, the first condition is to listen to society and talk with it.

An example of this is provided by the Danish firm Novo Nordisk, which is a global leader in the treatment of diabetes (Novo Nordisk, 2003b; Morsing and Thyssen, 2003). When it is confronted, for strategic decisions, with dilemmas that arise from complexity and uncertainty, it consults external personalities who can shed a different and even antagonistic light on the matter. To illustrate these dilemmas it cites the following questions:

- How can one reconcile the spirit of innovation and the principle of prudence in the management of risk?
- How can one improve the treatment of diabetes in poor countries while remaining profitable?
- How can one convince shareholders that sustainable development is necessary?

Questioning, even radical questioning, is not act of treason against the firm, it is a normal citizen's right. Debate is now more necessary than ever, for we do not know what is the common good in a world that is so complex and changing.

An adult and objective debate between 'those of Davos' and 'those of Porto Alegre' is essential. Any rejection of this risks a return to the eternal dialogue of the deaf between conservatives, reformers and more extreme radicals.

Do we have the time to face up to ideologies at length and to handle the dialogue on these matters at the level of anathema, imprecation and demonization? Is it not urgent to commit ourselves to concrete action? As we shall see, the movement for corporate social responsibility and some NGOs have begun to do this.

New forms of consultation

Engaging in debate and questioning is an important point of departure, but we must go further and try to organize it and participate in it in a systematic way. To do this it is necessary to broaden the current frameworks for consultation.

Professional associations play a very active part in social consultation. In many countries they are truly representative of their constituents. They therefore enjoy great legitimacy and the agreements they make have almost the force of law. But they usually restrict themselves to dialogue with unions and governments.

Moreover, by their very nature they are inclined to defend the positions that please the majority of their members, who are very diverse and scarcely united. They are not equipped to take *avant-garde* positions or to innovate in a radical manner. Nonetheless they have sometimes acted in a creative and spectacular way, for example in Europe at the time of the big agreements on social security and the sharing out of the fruits of productivity. Another example is the responsible care programme, thanks to which the chemical industry is committed to dealing with environmental problems in a more transparent and concerted way (see Smets, 2002). It is clear that useful progress is already being made through this method of consultation. But if we want to find a sustainable development model and persuade firms play an innovative and proactive role in it, we will have to broaden the processes of dialogue and cooperation, or even create new ones.

Broadened consultation will provide a powerful means of escaping from the single thought and 'de-enclaving' our economic model by opening it up to the great problems and aspirations of our age. Such consultations should include discussions of the main challenges of today and the future: a suitable development model for a globalizing world, the applications of new scientific knowledge, participation in the structures of world governance, levelling out the competitive game, orientating the market economy towards the common good of the planet, and so on. This approach must of course go beyond the national framework, and it is already beginning to take shape at the level of international and regional institutions.

While the size and complexity of the problems prevent us from advancing very quickly, structures are being put in place and firms can play an important part in this. This is the case with the Global Compact, set up by Kofi Annan, the World Business Council for Sustainable Development and Transparency International. The Johannesburg Conference in 2002 was marked by recognition of the essential role of the firm in the formulation of a sustainable development model. More than 160 multinationals were involved and some 100 chief executives took part (Chaveau and Rosé, 2003). When preparing for this conference the French committee recommended:

• Facilitating the adoption of social responsibilities by all French players by offering to all participants a framework for permanent meetings.
• The participation of French players in an international social and societal model that would integrate French and European specificities (Services du Premier Ministre, 2002).

We can therefore see that new forms of consultation are slowly being put in place, but in addition to the traditional representatives the consultations should include NGOs, scientific researchers and individuals who are concerned with meaning, ethics and purpose, such as philosophers and theologians.

In this regard a promising initiative has just been launched in Europe. The European Multi-Stakeholder Forum, created by CSR Europe and the European Commission, brings together the usual social partners (employers and unions) plus newcomers to consultation: NGOs and representatives of the movement of responsible firms. Its purpose is to consider the elements of a new development model and identify actions that can be taken by stakeholders to make the system more responsible. Twelve round tables are planned. These will have 50 participants, including university experts and civil servants.

There is evidence here of a will to maintain a European model, despite the pressures of the neoliberal globalization that the Anglo-Saxon model tends to impose.

Is there not a danger that such initiatives will replace action with endless palaver? The traditional business leaders think so. They believe that lengthy debates and talking shops serve no purpose, save to impede their actions, curb their dynamism and diminish their creativity. This scepticism must be fought. In an uncertain, complex and dangerous world, debate is preferable to lobbying.

In the current ethical and political vacuum the problems of purpose, values and power must be addressed and solutions found to the challenges of the future, rather than maintaining the inertia brought about by the single thought. From a democratic standpoint this constitutes the return of politics. The firm will only be truly responsible if it commits itself to consultation on essential matters. The questions posed by globalization and the technosciences are of major importance to our future, although as yet there is no obvious answer to them. Entrepreneurs, financiers and the markets cannot be the only directors of economic evolution, even though it is their specific domain of action. Sustainable development concerns all people, it is part of the public domain. In order to decide on the type of society we are to create together we must listen to all those who have something to say.

A person can simultaneously busy himself with his own affairs and those of the state; and even when different people are busy with different occupations they can pronounce on public matters without any inconvenience ... We consider someone who takes no part to be a useless citizen rather than simply a quiet one; and by ourselves we judge and reason as necessary on the questions; for in our eyes speech is not an obstacle to action: on the contrary, what is an obstacle is not to be first enlightened through speech before embarking on the action to be taken. (Thucydides)

The 'procedural approach' offers promising prospects in this regard. Developed by the German philosopher Jürgen Habermas (1987, 1992), it aims to organize systematically the methods and forms of consultation.

In a pluralist world such as ours, the appropriateness of a normative device (a rule or a decision) lies not only in its conformity to an ideal-type (for example a pre-established system of values) but also in the way in which this rule or decision has been established. Such an approach is designed to ensure that all those involved (the stakeholders) agree on the debating procedure before beginning to discuss the content. It offers a practical path for the renewal or improvement of democracy (Cobbaut, 1997) and to prevent the system from crushing the players.

The return of a political culture to the firm is necessitated by the fact that the firm is not an island. We belong to a democracy and the evolution of our development model must have the support of the people. Broadened consultation will make a strong contribution to this:

> Because we have received the power to convince ourselves mutually and make the object of our decisions appear clearly to us, not only are we freed from the primitive life, we have also become sufficiently united to build cities; we have established laws; we have discovered the arts; and for almost all our inventions it is speech that has allowed us to bring them to a good conclusion. (Isocrates, *Sur l'Echange*, quoted in de Romily, 1992)

Speech and debate are the foundations of a civilized life and general progress in society.

Transparency and evaluation

Secrecy has for long prevailed in the world of business: future projects, research programmes, strategies of persuasion and lobbying, executives' pay, information on possible negative consequences of decisions – all these are generally concealed, and when a scandal or a badly managed mistake comes to light, everything is done to smother it. In a competitive world, secrecy is acceptable in the case of strategy or research – Hannibal said he would burn his tunic if his battle plans were written on it. But it is unacceptable when it involves actions that might affect society as a whole or destroy the trust needed for the smooth operation of a market economy.

For a long time legislatures have decreed rules for financial and accounting transparency. These are aimed at enabling investors and lenders to trust the figures and information published by firms.

When firms are managed by honest people these mechanisms work well, or as well as human affairs can work. However during market booms there may be excesses, cheating and the falsification of balance sheets, as evidenced by the recent scandals in the US and to a lesser extent in Europe. The financial authorities then intervene to correct or replace the rules, even at the risk of going too far.

This type of transparency is obviously very important, but it is no longer sufficient. The requirement for transparency now extends well beyond accounting figures. Given the deviations of our development model, the new political conscience demands greater transparency in domains that are fundamental to our future, including the environment, science and technology, human rights and social justice.

Hence firms are being required to reveal much more than their financial affairs. They are expected to be explicit about potential risks posed by their products, the way in which they develop their workforce, the measures they intend to take to protect the environment, and how much they pay their executives.

This is a new type of culture for most firms that wish to be responsible, but the more enlightened ones have been committed to it for some years. This is directly in line with the evolution of debate and the new types of consultation. There can be no serious debate without transparency.

If transparency and openness had existed before, the damage caused by cigarettes would doubtless have been denounced earlier. As it was the large firms in this sector lied for 50 years in order to increase their sales, to the detriment of public health. Today the requirement for openness has increased considerably in sectors that can have an impact on health, the environment, human rights and so on. This is especially true of the food industry, the chemical and pharmaceutical sectors and the arms industry.

'Tools' of openness are beginning to be introduced. The 'triple balance sheet' – traditional accounting plus social and green accounting – is used by a growing number of large firms, some of which publish reports on sustainable development. International norms and basic principles for this have been established, for example the 2002 Sustainability Reporting Guidelines proposed by Global Reporting and the AA1000 Framework.

The majority of large firms have made an effort to improve their reporting transparency in these domains and to establish a database of the facts and figures that are necessary to debate and consultation. However, many researchers and NGOs have been very critical of these reports, claiming that there has been no independent verification, they contain insufficient numerical data and bases for comparison, there is little reference to the unions and collective negotiation, and so on. The most critical would impose standard formats and detailed contents on these reports and create auditing systems analogous to those in the field of accounting. As we shall see later, it is advisable to be wary of approaches that are too rigid and one-size-fits-all in a world that is rapidly evolving and whose creativity depends largely on individual initiatives.

Recall that the essence is not in the communication instrument or the audit structure, but in the spirit of concrete practices. In this domain the tool quickly becomes a ritual and it will not suffice. It may even be counterproductive if the firm does not subscribe to actions for a wider purpose and from a new ethical and political perspective.

We can mention here the very dynamic work by Transparency International against corruption. This movement succeeded in getting together a sufficiently large number of large firms to convince their countries' governments to sign the OECD convention that has made all forms of corruption illegal. Many of these firms have signed agreements between themselves to prevent such practices.

New governance?

Is it necessary to transform the power structures of firms and impose new methods of management and control on organizations geared to risk taking, innovation and creativity?

There have been numerous studies on this subject. In the majority of industrialized countries, commissions have been created, debates launched and reports written, including the Cadbury Report 1992 in the UK, Vienot 1999 in France, Lippens, 2005, in Belgium and Jaap Winter's report 2002 to the European Commission. In the US the Sarbanes–Oxley Act of 2002, reinforcing the legal constraints on corporate governance, voted in after the recent scandals, has given rise to considerable analysis and comment. It has strengthened controls and sanctions and might influence legislation in a number of countries.

These new moves are so disparate that the EU is considering whether it might be advisable to harmonize them to open the way to a 'shareholders' democracy'. The aim of this chapter is not to analyze the content of these moves, but simply to put them into the perspective of the new political culture of the responsible firm.

Once again we recall that the essence lies more in the spirit and behaviour of the players than in structures and controls. What matters is to organize the exercise of power in the firm so that the latter retains its dynamism but there are sufficient counterbalances to prevent the deviations associated with dominant executives: personalization of power, excessive centralization, rejection of questioning and controls, various forms of abuse and so on. Such deviations put the firm at risk of embarking on excessive acquisitions, making other large mistakes and even being subject to abuse of power or serious dishonesty. These deviations were discussed in Part I of this book.

To tackle the question of the governance of the firm we must return to the necessary balance between the principal decision makers, what economists refer to as agency theory (Jensen and Meckling, 1976). This can be summarized as follows.

Early in the history of capitalism, professional managers were appointed by employers, often the founders of the firm, to help them manage what was becoming a complex organization. The subsequent dilution of capital and the growing number of shareholders made the part played by these managers more crucial and necessitated the establishment (via negotiations) of clear rules on the relationship between powers of these two groups of players.

According to Peter Martin's (2002) excellent summary, balance can be achieved by adhering to the following set of rules: professionals should manage the firm in the interests of the shareholders, under the supervision of the board of directors, within the framework of clear and accepted accounting principles, and sharing the results (profits) in a reasonable manner between the parties.

This form of power sharing has been effective for a long time and has ensured the growth and improved performance of many Western firms. However several of the components have been put into question by the recent scandals, prompting a wave of proposals to change the structures of management. The majority of these proposals are aimed repositioning shareholders at the centre of operations, returning to them a sort of sovereignty over the firm and protecting them against possible excesses by or incompetence of professional managers.

This is in line with the financial aims of the firm (shareholder value) and does not deal with the influence of firms on our collective future or with the cultural transformations necessary to make firms more responsible. This type of reform only concerns ethics at their most basic level (honesty) and will contribute little to sustainable development.

By proposing to counterbalance the power of professional directors by increasing that of shareholders or their representatives, the 'new governance' is principally focusing on protecting investors against the excesses of directors. This may restore confidence in the capital markets and improve the running of the economy, but it does not directly address the major challenges raised in this book or the new forms of consultation discussed in this chapter. Cobbaut and Lenoble (2003) have written a critical analysis of the overly financial emphasis and limitations of the new governance. They propose a new institutional approach that will open the way to the new forms of dialogue discussed here.

In this new trend of corporate governance, certain points need to be stressed because they may bring about a change in behaviour in respect of honesty and transparency.

Independent administrators will be able to question all forms of collusion (cocooning) between professional directors and certain shareholder representatives; they will be able to counterbalance the excessive power of overly autonomous executives, question professional managers and limit errors.

The existence of a strong audit committee within the board of directors goes in the same direction: it should supervise such matters as executives' remuneration, share options and the accuracy of figures.

Another interesting recommendation is to make it less difficult for members of staff publicly to denounce bad practices, behaviour or decisions that infringe internal rules, the ethical code or simple honesty.

At the heart of the structural reforms there is the role of the 'boss' (managing director, CEO, top manager). Some want to reduce the powers of the boss by putting him or her under the control of a board presided over and dominated by independent external administrators. In my view this is unrealistic and stems from wishful thinking.

The asymmetry of information is such that a director will always have a distinct advantage over the external administrator. The most important thing is to create a climate of trust between those who incarnate entrepreneurial drive, initiatives and action and those who are responsible for controlling them, advising them and looking after the overall internal and external balancing of the whole.

To return to the *raison d'être* and purpose of firms, it is the chief executives who are responsible; it is they, with their teams, who have the power to integrate all the interests of the participants and include their firms' strategies in a wider vision of the common good and the future of society. It is down to them to propose this difficult synthesis, to negotiate it with the firms' administrators and shareholders and to sell it to the financial analysts.

If the aims and purpose of the firm are broadened, if the ethics of the future and the new political culture are put in place, they will be more effective than a change of structure or control tools.

We should add that the extensive research carried out in this area has so far found no link between forms of governance and the profitability or strategic performance of the firm. Moreover if one wishes to link sustainable development with governance of the firm, it will be necessary to explain further the *raison d'être* and purpose of the latter (Van den Berghe, 2003).

The use of power

The cultural evolution of the responsible firm touches closely on the conception that executives and managers have of their power and the way they exert it (de Woot, 1998).

To simplify in the extreme, one might suggest that there exist two principal concepts of power: the power of domination, which consists in dominating the game in order to control it better; and the power of service, which consists in leading and coordinating the efforts of all in a common project. These two orientations create quite different cultures in the firm.

The power of domination often leads to a strong personalization of power, to unilateral views such as *salus firmae suprema lex* (let the welfare of the firm be the final law), to over-risky adventures and cynical behaviour: little attention to society, indifference, manipulation, secrecy, and undervaluing and sometimes scorning people.

Conversely the power of service encourages participation and membership, attention to the common good, transparency, communication, respect, knowledge and motivation.

These two models are clearly polar extremes but they illustrate the diversity of corporate culture. As always, one must go beyond the sketches and add the subtleties of life.

Contrasting the power of domination with the power of service underlines the traditional distinction between the cynic and the humanist. The one recommends a realistic morality of power, the other an ideal of civilization. The one considers power in its instrumental logic: the means that command the ends and control action. The other makes the exercise of power a branch of ethics: this implies a moral responsibility and submission to fundamental values.

For the first, the universe is a jungle and men are dangerous. One must be constantly on guard and 'politics is as far removed from morality as are mathematics, like war or chess, it authorizes any ruse or strategy' (Margolin, 1967). It is the universe of Machiavelli, the jurists of Philippe le Bel or Emperor Che-Huang-Ti. 'One governs men with one's head. One does not play chess with a good heart' (Chamfort).

For the second, politics arises from morality. One cannot separate the exercise of power from a concept of society based on respect for mankind and the support of those directed for the plans of the directors. Advocates of the power of service believe that the world can be civilized because mankind and societies are perfectible. This is the universe of Erasmus, Montesquieu, Aristotle, Confucius and the Bible. It is the aim of every democratic regime. 'Politics is the art of commanding free men' (Aristotle).

If the firm wishes to base its actions on a vision of the common good, it will have to adopt or develop the concept of power as a service. This is consistent with the new purpose and ethics for the future. It is also consistent with the methods of consultation to be put in place to confront the challenges of globalization.

The proper use of power is essential to the cultural evolution of the firm. But it will be difficult to change because business leaders rarely explicitly recognize the reality of power. They rarely admit that power is not based entirely on reason but also stems from passion. 'Power is a drug', I was told by one director – a contemporary echo of a thousand-year-old truth. 'This appetite for domination, among all the passions of mankind, is the most intoxicating' (Saint Augustine).

'I place in the first rank, as a general tendency of the whole of humanity, a perpetual and unceasing desire to acquire power and more power' (Hobbes).

When we speak of power, those who hold it modestly lower their gaze. For them it conjures up leadership, management and direction. But the raw reality of power – ambition, conquest, intrigue and *Raison d'Etat* – is not revealed. It is as though it is a distasteful topic, one that is indecent and dangerous. Human beings do not like to talk about their passions.

However they do invoke the constraints of an economic and technical system of which they are not masters and which imposes on them rules to be followed on pain of extinction. Knowing how to play by the rules and finding this stimulating, satisfying and the provider of professional justification, they become addicted to the game and do not see its limitations and malfunctionings. Whereas the most enlightened business leaders try to transform the system, the more conservative lock themselves into the single thought. They use their power to defend the model that they serve to drive, and they lack the will to make it evolve, thereby abdicating their responsibility as citizens. This is why there is still so much inertia in the system:

> Several were... very clever people in their profession; they possessed full knowledge of all the details of administration... but as for the great science of government, which teaches an understanding of the general movement of society, a judgement of what happens in the minds of the masses and a foresight of what will result from it, they were as new to it as the people themselves... Their minds were therefore fixed on the point of view that had been reached by their fathers... In those places where assemblies preserve their ancient constitution without changing anything, they stop the progress of civilization rather than assist it. One might say that they are foreign and impervious to the new spirit of the age. (Tocqueville)

9
The Move Towards Social Responsibility

Take an active part, do not resign yourself to events, do not let yourself slide into the flood that carries all away.

(Mirabeau)

Myth or reality?

When companies describe themselves as responsible and announce this publicly, should we take them seriously? Are they just mouthing slogans and pious aspirations on engaging in image building, or are we witnessing an emerging reality and the possibility of concrete action?

The central thesis of this chapter is that the firm can only become responsible and promote sustainable development if it transforms itself profoundly: by broadening its *raison d'être* and purpose, by adopting more ethical behaviour and by engaging in a true debate on improving our development model.

Our observation of companies suggests that some are resolutely committed to this course, and therefore such an evolution is possible. But will there be enough of these companies to push back the single thought and transform the system? It is too soon to say, but a fundamental move has begun.

What can be highlighted here is the appearance of a new type of enterprise, one that goes beyond purely instrumental logic and is concerned with the problems of society. We shall look at four examples: Lafarge, a world leader in construction materials, Shell in the energy field, Daimler-Chrysler in the transport sector, and Novo Nordisk, a Danish pharmaceutical firm specializing in drugs to combat diabetes.

Despite the scandal about the overestimation of its oil reserves, we have included Shell among our examples for two reasons. First, for several years Shell has shown a real will to change its culture, behaviour and tools for the sake of the environment and sustainable development. Second, it provides an opportunity to reflect on the imperfections, instabilities and dangers that have threatened the evolution of the firm, despite its cultural transformation. Three Shell executives have resigned – including the chairman – who stand accused of exaggerating the extent of the firm's oil reserves. This is the subject of an investigation by the supervisory authority (the SEC or Securities and Exchange Commission) and the US Justice Department. The three directors are said to have lied in order to increase their chance of promotion or keeping their job. Due to inadequate mechanisms of supervision and control, the real facts remained concealed for two years. The firm's governance has therefore also been called into question. In the meantime an extensive structural and governance reform has been launched. Should this firm be kept in our sample? Let the reader be the judge. What we wish to show is that cultural change takes time and is never complete. No firm can be entirely immune from unacceptable practices. Is it therefore right to regard Shell's efforts to promote sustainable development as null and void? It is important to ask this question and consider the credibility of the company's collective effort despite individual failings.

Our purpose here is not to verify a working hypothesis, but to suggest that in certain cases firms do embrace social responsibility and go through the profound transformations described in this chapter. Such companies are characterized by four fundamental traits:

- They have enlarged their purpose and *raison d'être* to take into account the concept of sustainable development.
- They have blended these into their strategies, policies and practices.
- They have developed a culture of responsibility.
- They regard this evolution as a collective process that they cannot bring to a satisfactory conclusion by their efforts alone.

Broadened aims and purpose

The aims and purpose of the companies considered here have broadened to include the new dimensions of the globalizing world.

'We are convinced that an industrial group such as ours can only survive in the long term if it subscribes to a perspective of sustainable development', asserts Lafarge (2002a) in its annual report.

The companies in the Shell Group are also fully committed to this, but have no illusions about the difficulties that will have to be overcome. Shell points out that it was 'the first large energy firm to support publicly the Universal Declaration of Human Rights (U.N. 1948) and the concept of sustainable development' (Shell, 1998).

Daimler-Chrysler (2002) recommends a proactive stance: 'It is the social responsibilities of the firm that will open the way to sustainable development ... in the framework of the global partnership proposed at Rio with a view to creating a more secure and more prosperous future for all peoples of the world.'

Finally, Novo Nordisk (2003b) supports a vision aimed at future generations: sustainable development and a society built on trust, transparency, shared values and partnerships. 'In order to realize this vision, the firm has a role to play. It can create wealth and improve the quality of its products without damaging the planet.... The firm can use its collective creativity and expertise to help to resolve the problems of social injustice and inequality. Two elements focus our action: our commitment to create a difference (innovation) and to pursue a profitable and sustainable development.' What a fine example of a responsible spirit of enterprise.

In these four cases there is a publicly affirmed will to make economic progress serve a common good that directs and surpasses it. There is also a way of raising ethics beyond the questions of integrity and honesty.

Our point of departure is the fundamental ethical question: what world, what society do we wish to create together? The companies answer this unequivocally: 'a sustainable world' (Lafarge, 2002a). It is interesting to note that the broadening of their aims and purpose has released them from the imprisonment of the single thought, opened them up to new forms of consultation and changed their priorities.

> Our approach to sustainable development is based on the following ... :
>
> - opening up, dialogue and partnership;
> - creation of economic value;

- social progress;
- protection of the environment. (Lafarge, 2002b)

We have identified three priority areas to which our firm will devote itself:

- globalization, sustainable development and governance;
- evolution of the industry's role and the broadening of responsibilities;
- stakeholder demand for more transparency and accountability. (Novo Nordisk, 2003b)

Concrete implementation

The new vision is beginning to be translated into decisions and strategies. For example these companies have systematically implemented environmental policies and are beginning to address the negative effects of their activities:

- Lafarge, in partnership with the World Wildlife Fund, is reducing its emission of pollutant gases and restoring the sites of its quarries once the extractive activity has stopped.
- Daimler-Chrysler is directing its research efforts at the problems of pollution: cleaner paintwork, exhaust filtering, new engine fuel technologies, fuel-cell technology and so on.
- Shell, in cooperation with Greenpeace, is stepping up and improving its environmental policies. With Human Rights, it is working to improve respect for human rights in the countries in which it operates. It is also conducting research on alternative energy sources, waste treatment and so on.
- Novo Nordisk considers that the fight against diabetes is not only an economic strategy (a business proposition) but also implies more focused social research and better identification of areas in which it can make a concrete contribution.

These companies are also strengthening their participation in local community efforts: education, the fight against AIDS, the protection of natural sites, the creation of nature reserves and so on.

Moreover they have absorbed their new purpose and responsibilities into their management tools, codes of behaviour and measurement of results. 'We have...deployed our [sustainable development] commitments at all levels of the organization: in our policies, in the operational objectives of the main divisions...[and] in the new *Advance* programme of the cement branch' (Collomb, 2002b).

At Novo Nordisk the 'management methods integrate at every level its commitment to sustainable development, from the board of directors via the operational units to individual employees. This constitutes a quite robust management system through which strategic objectives, targets to be achieved and performance indicators are defined, pursued and evaluated' (Novo Nordisk, 2003b).

These measures have become normal components of management. They are beginning to be made concrete in tools such as the triple balance sheet (economic, social and environmental accounting). Detailed reports are published, and independent auditing mechanisms have been put in place to guarantee objective analysis and increase credibility.

Prior culture

For each of the four companies, the transformation of their activities has been aided by a very strong prior culture, shared by the managers and widely communicated to the staff.

For years Lafarge has followed a participative model that encourages decentralized responsibility. In 1977, on the initiative of Olivier Lecerf (1991), action principles were defined and since then these have directed the firm; in the pursuit of improved performance they give a central place to people and respect for the general interest. These principles are periodically reviewed and adapted to new situations and the evolution of the group. They have created an ethical culture, responsibility for the environment and a capacity for self-questioning (de Woot and Winterscheid, 1997).

Shell has gone through a similar process. In 1976 it defined its general business principles and has since reviewed them regularly to take account of changes in the environment. These principles include a code of conduct that is designed to aid those who have to take difficult decisions. The principles are intended to facilitate the implementation of social responsibilities.

However their existence did not enable Shell to avoid the virulent public protests sparked by its proposed sinking of the Brent Spar oil platform and its allegedly too passive role in Nigeria where it is heavily invested when Nigerian militants were sentenced to death and executed. In the wake of these difficulties a fundamental transformation was planned. This involved consulting 7500 people in 10 countries, 1300 opinion leaders and 600 Shell employees in 55 countries in order to find ways of adapting to the new challenges and to reorient Shell's responsibilities in a more complex, more anti-establishment and more paradoxical world.

The same goes for Daimler-Chrysler, which, in line with the Rhineland model of codetermination, has long tried to ensure social responsibility by looking for possible convergences between economic performance and requirements for the common good.

For more than 10 years Novo Nordisk has been guided by a vision of sustainable development. It has adopted the triple balance sheet approach (economic, social and environmental accounting), which 'has helped us to define our interactions with the stakeholders: shareholders, diabetes sufferers, health professionals, employees, suppliers, local communities, NGOs, governments, public authorities and any other group that is likely to be affected by our actions or influenced by them' (Novo Nordisk, 2003b).

These action principles, 'the Novo Nordisk way of management' are reflected in the company's culture, defined in a charter and translated into concrete policies on bioethics, health, security, patents, staff, the environment and so on.

Ongoing process

The four companies view the transition towards a model of social responsibility as a process. Listening to others, in-depth analyses, the adoption of new measurement tools, ongoing training in these areas and partnerships – all these are part of a long-term process that depends on a will to learn and to change:

> For a firm like Lafarge, advancement on the path of sustainable development is like a marathon race: the public would like to see a lightning departure, worthy of a 100 metre sprint, but we must resist this temptation, in order to be able to sustain our effort in the long term. This approach seem less spectacular, but we believe it [is] more effective. (Collomb, 2002b)

One of the principal elements of this process is systematic training in the new culture. Lafarge's 'Leader for Tomorrow' project is aimed at strengthening both the culture of responsibility in and the performance of the group.

For Novo Nordisk the current challenge is to embed its new responsibilities into all its practices and management methods. Merely announcing values and policies is not sufficient, it is essential to apply them correctly and this is an endless process.

The same goes for the new threats and opportunities in the fields of health and the environment. Novo Nordisk has three permanent committees to attend to these matters. External experts are invited to present their views and comments on the ethical, scientific and economic dilemmas that arise within the firm's strategic framework. Just being able to debate with these individuals and show them that certain questions can only be dealt with through dialogue increases the chance of instilling mutual trust, which is the source of cooperation. Novo Nordisk also asks its collaborators to develop scenarios for a better future and to suggest means of securing these.

Another important element of the process is cooperation with NGOs. For example Shell, cooperates with two important NGOs: Greenpeace for environmental matters and Human Rights for questions of human rights. It consults them during the preparation of plans and includes them in the examination of the results of actions.

Lafarge has formed a partnership with the World Wildlife Fund (WWF), the first partnership entered into by the latter with an industrial group under its 'Conservation Partner' programme. The partnership involves commitments in three areas:

• The establishment of environmental performance indicators.
• The establishment of high standards for the reclamation of quarry sites, particularly in relation to biodiversity.
• The establishment of a programme for a reduction in CO_2 emissions.

Another part of the process of change is participation in international efforts. Novo Nordisk plays an active part in international debates on sustainable development and the new responsibilities of the pharmaceutical sector. For instance it has attended the World Economic Forum (held each year in Davos) and the World Summit on Sustainable Development in Johannesburg. It is a signatory to important international agreements, such as the Charter for Sustainable Development, the UN Convention on Biological Diversity (1992), the Universal Declaration of Human Rights and the Global Compact.

Lafarge is very involved in the 'Towards a Sustainable Cement Industry' programme (2002) of the World Business Council for Sustainable Development, which outlines the targets towards which the cement industry must advance. The importance of this programme is illustrated by the fact that this industry is one of the main producers of CO_2 emissions.

Finally, we should mention the promotion and publicizing of these companies' new culture to other companies in their industries. They are seriously committed to the improvement of the current development model, and there can be no doubting the sincerity of their leaders, whose efforts cannot be put down to a simple public relations exercise. The quality of decision making, the tradition of these companies and the visibility of their remedial actions are such that one would have to be malicious or ill-informed to doubt their commitment, values and political will.

The commitment of these companies is based on solid convictions. They are major players in the economic system and feel responsible for its evolution. They believe they can contribute through their capacity for action and creativity. They are convinced that this evolution is necessary because the current development model is losing its legitimacy.

One can therefore state that the will of certain companies to assume social responsibility is a concrete reality and that it is happening through a change in their culture and purpose. The questions that should now be asked are as follows. Is this movement becoming widespread? Will it last? Will it be sufficient to correct the defects of a globalizing market economy that is poorly regulated at the international level?

General movement?

As we have seen, many initiatives have been taken by companies that have not waited for public regulations to begin to evolve in the directions indicated in this book. The pressures of society and the intelligent anticipation of some business leaders have set off a transformation.

Depending on the sector and the size of the companies in question, there have been many statements of interest in the environment, human rights, product safety, accounting accuracy, new forms of governance, sustainable development and so on.

New types of association have been formed, such as partnerships between companies and NGOs, and the participation of a few large companies in international actions such as the Global Compact, launched by the secretary general of the UN, Kofi Annan, in 1999. Associations of important companies are campaigning in favour of sustainable development, including Corporate Social Responsibility Europe and the US, and Business in the Community in the UK. Some international companies are also active in the World Business Council for Sustainable Development, which includes 160 multinationals representing 10–15 per cent of world turnover, and the International Chamber of Commerce. These two organizations set up the Business Action for Sustainable Development, to represent business in Johannesburg (Chaveau and Rosé, 2003).

There are many more such initiatives, details of which can be found in recent publications (see especially ibid.). Voluntary change is therefore beginning to emerge on the part of companies, but are there enough of them to bring about an evolution of the development model? The most enthusiastic players proclaim that the movement is irreversible and that the balance is beginning to swing in favour of sustainable development. However even if the most enlightened companies – those which understand the threats – are moving forward and are attempting to take others with them, scepticism and resistance to change are still formidable.

Other companies are stepping on the bandwagon without understanding that it involves a profound change. They think it is all about public relations. They learn the vocabulary, adopt a few rituals or ethical codes, but continue as before. There are also many conservative business people who are locked into their instrumental logic and for whom the language of social responsibility is double Dutch. 'Few people are wise enough to prefer the blame that is useful to them to the praise that betrays them' (La Rochefoucauld).

Let us not underestimate the degree of resistance by the economic system itself and the pressure it exerts on companies. If a firm as responsible as IBM says it is forced by the system to practise relocation and subcontracting against its will, one can see the limits of the evolution towards social responsibility.

Our competitors are already practising this religion [relocation].
One of our challenges is to find a balance between what the firm
has to do and the impact that this may have on people. And this
area is one of those where this type of dilemma strikes us full-force.
Our competitors do it; we are therefore obliged to do it too (human
resources director at IBM, quoted in Roberts and Luce, 2003).

We should also recall the power of investment funds and pension
funds. If these continue to be guided by traditional criteria they will
present a major obstacle to the evolution of the development model.
Monks (2003) defends the idea that, because of their global investments, these institutions could exert a decisive influence on business
leaders. 'They are well placed to impose basic rules (new criteria) for
the investment of their funds. They would then be capable of initiat-
ing change in those countries that dragged their feet' in this area.
Several ethical funds have been established, but they only represent
an infinitesimal part of the sector and their results are not yet
impressive.

But there is more. What is needed is a cultural change, and many
companies do not understand this.

Nonetheless successful companies are used to change – strategic,
technical and organizational – because their survival depends on it.
The pressure of competition and the evolution of the markets has
forced them to adapt constantly and to react quickly to threats and
opportunities. The most successful of them have turned their capacity
for change into a major competitive weapon. But in the area that
concerns us another type of change is required – a change of attitude
and purpose.

Caught up in the race to win the competition, dominated by a
single thought and unsupported by coherent global legislation on
sustainable development, many companies have not yet extended
their capacity for change to ethical and political change.

However the four examples presented above show that such a
change is possible. If other firms want to assume social responsibility
they will have to undergo a similar transformation.

Such change is complex and takes time. First, change is always
difficult. Resistance and obstacles are encountered at every level of
the organization: scepticism, poor perception of external problems,
lack of vision by managers, heavy workloads preventing listening

and debate, defence of positions and interests, fear of losing decision-making powers and so on.

All change requires a considerable effort and a real will to overcome resistance. Quality leadership at all levels and a culture of consultation, dialogue and questioning are the best weapons here.

Change is less difficult and carried out better when it is done 'cold', that is, before it is necessitated by a crisis. A negotiated change is often more effective than an imposed change. When a problem or a challenge is identified in time it can be handled with a view to the long term using the best resources of the present. The economic system has been allowed to slide into deviation, but the most aware companies are already progressing towards sustainable development. They have done this in a sufficiently voluntary way to retain control and to find a balance between economic performance and social responsibility.

Second, change is a complex process and to succeed it must be undertaken and managed in a systematic way. There are necessary preconditions to ensure that this process is able to overcome resistance along the way:

- A pressure for urgency: external pressure from society or the environment, but above all internal pressure – questioning, rejection of self-satisfaction, sensitivity to criticism and weak signals.
- A shared vision to ensure the convergence of efforts and the mobilization of energy, and to orientate the organization towards the future rather than back to the past.
- The wherewithal for evolution: sufficient resources, better use of existing resources and above all proactive leaders at every level of the organization.
- Concrete programmes to show that change is possible.

If one of the above is absent or weak, the process of change is blocked. The key to managing change does not lie in paying attention to each element separately but in linking one to the other and treating them as a whole.

Finally, there is opposition to cultural change from the 'high priests' of the 'market religion': professors of management, management gurus, economists, editors of journals and financial analysts, who day after day influence thinking, train the young and promote the 'truths' of neoliberal globalization.

Let us consider the business schools. These could become major agents for cultural change if they transformed themselves and addressed the challenges faced by the current development model. But their self-assurance, not to say their arrogance, says a lot about their will to question themselves: 'the way that we teach is by far the best for training in management and leadership', the dean of a large management school said recently (*Financial Times*, 28 April 2003).

Their influence is vast. Not only do they train, retrain and recycle the majority of CEOs and managers of large companies, they also impose and widely promote their vision of the firm and their philosophy of management.

It is their management culture that is transmitted and their former students remain imbued with it as they rise in the hierarchy and take control of companies.

It is they who produce the authors of the most widely read management texts, the gurus, wise men and consultants of every hue who besiege the firm. Most follow the American model and their teaching has become very uniform.

Although this could be seen as an extreme view, I would venture to suggest that many management schools are unsuitable for the new challenges of our time, for several reasons. The most important reason is their imprisonment in the single thought, that is, the hard-line neoliberal model. This often forms the basis of their teaching and is virtually never called into question. They may be outraged by business scandals but they do not discuss the fundamental flaws in the model. There are few if any business schools that ask their students the ethical question of our time: what kind of world should we build with the resources, creativity and power available to us?

The *raison d'être* of management schools is to equip their students to operate the existing system in an effective way without concerning themselves with its purpose and defects, or the dangers that it is beginning to present. In this sense the majority of professors are the thurifers of an ideology, the clerics and celebrants of the single thought. They present a major obstacle to the establishment of a true culture of sustainable development.

These schools defend an outdated model that is losing its legitimacy and that enlightened companies are now questioning, 'What is taught in the majority of American business schools, if not in all, constitutes an indoctrination in the never-questioned ideology of the maximization of the shareholder's wealth' (Ellsworth, 2002). This also applies to the majority of European management schools:

> After 36 years in the world of education, including 15 at Stanford, I am persuaded that the business schools, given their influence on the thinking and behaviour of managers, ought to question the values that they promote, the vision of the firm that they propose, as well as the concept of the society that is written into their theories, their models, their methods and their tools for management.[1]

The second reason for the unsuitableness of management schools, is that, locked as they are into their ideology, they do little to prepare their students to face up to their social responsibilities and the real challenges of the twenty-first century: evolution of human societies and new forms of contestation, the questionable legitimacy of economic and financial power, broadening the purpose of the firm, ethics for the future, new forms of societal debate, the use of prudence in the application of science and technology, and so on.

Apart from globalization, the majority of important contemporary trends are omitted from the culture they promote. This often leads them to be no more than vocational schools without a university dimension. They pass on technical skills, tools, decision-making methods and organizational methods rather than values, independent thinking and ethical concern. One cannot criticize them for imparting professional knowledge, but one can question their essentially instrumental approach, given that their students are destined to drive an economic and technical system that is increasingly being challenged. More critical still, according to Mintzberg they do not even prepare their students for the profession of management but are content to pass on specialist skills, such as marketing, finance and production.[2]

Of course there are some brilliant thinkers in their midst, but the latter are not representative of the culture of the schools. They are swimming against the tide and have not yet succeeded in opening up the schools to the social and human dimension (de Bettignies, 2002).

The schools are mostly technical institutions oriented towards a logic of efficiency without clear purpose. They carry out little research in the academic sense of the word. Their courses are mainly instrumental and applied. They seek to promote a system that they view uncritically.

As for specific teaching of social responsibility, a recent survey of 166 management schools clearly shows that such teaching is very undeveloped and is not part of their culture, despite students' interest in this topic.[3] On average, only 12 per cent of the world's business schools have a mandatory course entirely devoted to this area, although 32 per cent offer courses as an option. Only 20 per cent of schools allocate funds for research in this area.

It is therefore not surprising that they are resistant, as are many of the managers they have trained, to any fundamental change to the economic model and the ideology that underpins it. We should also not be surprised to learn that some of the recent deviations and scandals were perpetrated by former students of such schools.

Sumantra Ghoshal of the London Business School goes as far as to say that the content of their teaching has strengthened the deviation in behaviour that they so vociferously condemn. 'By basing themselves on negative and profoundly pessimistic assumptions about human beings and institutions, the pseudo-scientific theories of management have done much to strengthen, if not create, the pathological conduct of managers and companies' (Ghoshal, 2003).

This approach is reflected in the majority of publications, journals and seminars supported by the schools of management. For example the promotional literature of a large American management journal states that it will help you to build the future. Is this the new development model at last? Not at all – it is about making better use of intellectual property as a major competitive weapon, understanding the importance of 'narcissistic' leaders in transforming the firm, fighting against inertia and so on. These topics are not completely alien to our argument, but they remain at the level of means. One would expect the building of the future to involve discussions of the aims, values and sociopolitical evolution of the firm.

In 2003 the *Financial Times* (4–29 August) published 20 full pages on the evolution of management. Professors from business schools contributed articles or put forward the views of famous experts. The series began in an attractive way with an invitation never to stop thinking about tomorrow (London, 2003). But it was essentially about effectiveness and efficiency rather than the major evolutionary trends and a responsible vision for the future. Apart from one or two exceptions the features were on marketing, competition, quality, strategy, products and so on. The few articles that indirectly tackled the social responsibilities of the firm dealt with leadership and integrity. The dominant tone was of means rather than ends.

A new type of management school is required if the development model is to evolve. This is not the place to define what this school should be in order to serve as an agent for change, but some directions can be outlined.

It would begin by ceasing to teach the single thought. The priority is not so much to create numerous new courses as to abandon those that propagate the single thought (Ghoshal, 2003). They would of course continue to produce managers of a high professional standard, but they should be more academic.

In contrast to technical schools, universities teach basic concepts and not only the use of tools. They foster a critical mind and the capacity to stand back, refine the understanding of differences and promote the capacity to integrate with multicultural and often confrontational groups. They tend to train citizens and not just professionals. This is also the vision contained in a study on European education, produced jointly by the rectors of universities and chief executives of major companies (ERT and CRE, 1994).

The teaching and research of the new type of management school would address the major topics in social evolution: interdependence and solidarity, sustainable development, the ambiguities of the technosciences, the legitimacy or otherwise of private economic powers, new forms of governance, consultation and debate, and so on. The analysis of these and the responses by firms would not only happen through the use of tools and codes of practice that so often turn into rituals and instruments of public relations. They would take the form of profound reflection and a manner of thinking that would facilitate the forging of a new culture. The debate on values and responsibilities would become more central and better integrated into research projects and teaching programmes (de Bettignies, 2002).

The school's studies and research would be more multidisciplinary. If it was not integrated with a university, it could enter into a partnership or cooperative arrangement with one or more universities, which would themselves foster a broad multidisciplinary approach. The latter is essential to dealing with the challenges of our time and to build a model of the firm that meets the requirements of sustainable development.

Such a subject requires the knowledge and the convergence of various disciplines. The following are some examples:

- Shall one advocate a legal or a voluntary approach to the new responsibilities of the firm? This point must be examined in detail by lawyers. Only the law can explore the credibility of the 'soft laws' created by codes of conduct and company charters, or the suitability of the criteria for valuation and accountability. The same goes for everything that relates to the governance of the firm.
- World-wide regulation is necessary to establish and enforce the rules of competition in the global market and create a level playing field for firms. This new and very complex problem has to be dealt with by economists, political scientists, sociologists and lawyers. If firms are to make a contribution their managers must have a better understanding of what is involved.
- The potential long-term risks arising from new scientific discoveries and their technological and commercial exploitation cannot be studied without resort to moral philosophy, the sciences, economics, medicine and so on. This pertains for environmental problems, transgenic plants, cloning, drugs and so on.
- Dialogue and cooperation between firms and NGOs, must be tackled from the viewpoint of sociology and the political sciences. The same goes for the new forms of national, European and world-wide consultation.
- The establishment of a balance between the necessary rules and regulations to tame the market and the freedom for entrepreneurial initiative must be studied by management scientists and organizational theorists, as well as by economists, business lawyers and public lawyers.
- The relationship between the long-term performance of companies and their exercise of social responsibility necessitates the conducting

of case studies and a new conceptualization of the theory of the firm. This will require business schools and universities to work as a team.

We would stress the importance of philosophy in this.[4] At a time when we are questioning the purpose and meaning of economic progress, this discipline is more necessary than ever but few management schools have realized this.

'Philosophers differ from business professionals in that they contribute nothing concrete. They offer no assets and little knowledge, because their knowledge does not arise from a technique. Philosophy in the firm is aimed at making better sense of the meaning and *raison d'être* of economic games. It serves to shed light on the ways of thinking in the business world, which are mostly implicit. It invites us to mistrust the evidence and look beyond it. The most persistent bias of our century, the shadows that hide reality from us, are, according to the inspired intuition of Arthur Koestler, the screens of our measuring instruments and our computers:

> We need philosophers to get us out of the rut in which we are stuck.... Management needs a wisdom fashioned especially for it.... We need new philosophers to open our eyes and make us see the reality of today with a new and inventive eye. (de Brabandére *et al.*, 2000)

Breakthroughs have been made in this direction, but rarely in management schools, apart from the efforts of some innovative professors who are not deeply integrated into the culture of the schools. In the past MIT did adopt an approach of this kind in its programmes for executives. They had to read and discuss three classic texts: *Antigone* (Sophocles), for questions about the limits of power, *The Prince* (Machiavelli), for the purpose of effective action, and *The Red and the Black* (Stendhal), for ambition and the conduct of one's life.

More recently a Brussels training and consultancy firm, Philosophie et Management, has organized annual seminars on philosophy for high-level executives. This training clearly meets a demand because it has aroused considerable enthusiasm and has been very successful.

In a rapidly accelerating information society, responsibility will increasingly depend on wisdom and reflection. T. S. Eliot (1948) had a premonition of this when he wrote:

Where is the Life we have lost in living?
Where is the wisdom we have lost in knowledge?
Where is the knowledge we have lost in information?

In this disrupted and unsustainable system, is it not essential to rediscover life and wisdom?

We would be deluding ourselves if we believed that management schools, as they stand at the moment, are capable of shedding light on the social responsibility of the firm. However their very survival might depend on their ability to do so. One commentator has gone as far as to predict that in the future they will become like Jurassic Park (de Bettignies, 2002). It is interesting to note that the most advanced business leaders are exerting the pressure on them to change, but their culture is such that many of them do not understand what is involved. According to one business leader, if the management schools do not adapt quickly, companies will do without them (Davignon, 2002).

Sustainable development?

Researchers have not yet been able to establish a link between the practice of social responsibility and economic performance. What can be said is that the majority of companies that have adopted a sustainable development model have been successful at the economic level. Thus it can be inferred that a successful firm can also be a responsible firm, although not necessarily more successful than one that is not responsible. One might suggest that economic success is a condition for social success (see Van den Berghe, 2002, 2003).

What would happen if an economic downturn, not to mention a real recession, were to erode the profitability of responsible companies and force them to take short-term measures that were incompatible with sustainable development? Without the creation of a level playing field, there is a risk to see corporate social responsibilities doomed to remain a fair weather policy (Defraigne, 2004).

Would an economic slump endanger their strategies to safeguard the environment, develop human resources or research useful, but as yet unprofitable, alternative products? Would the survival imperative cause firms to halt the responsible activities they embarked on voluntarily during a period of prosperity? Let us go further. If international competition is not evened out – a level playing field established – will more aggressive and less responsible companies attempt to create comparative advantages for themselves by practising a kind of social and environmental dumping? The pressures of competition would then be so strong that they might impose constraints on responsible firms. However the most enlightened firms seem to believe that they will be able to resist such pressures if the new responsibilities have been properly integrated into their culture and purpose.

Novo Nordisk considers that its commitment must be for the long term because sustainable development can only succeed in the long term. 'In fifteen years, we have known highs and lows. That makes things more difficult, but we have continued because responsibilities are part of our culture' (Kingo, 2003). 'During 2002, our values were put to the test, as well as our capacity to produce an adequate profit for our shareholders. . . . However, we made no compromises on our values or on our commitment to integrate the triple balance sheet (economic, social and political) into our manner of conducting the firm' (Novo Nordisk, 2003b).

One would like to think that when firms' purpose has been broadened, culture transformed and transparency assured, they will have furnished themselves with constraints that will guarantee a certain permanence in their approach; that is, once they go beyond a certain threshold it will be difficult for them to go back.

One can also envisage that political and societal evolution towards a sustainable development model will underpin the early efforts of the most enlightened companies and contribute to the transformation of social responsibility into a condition for the long-term success and profitability of firms. In this event the sustainability of the movement will be more likely.

For the time being we can only suggest a working hypothesis: if a firm integrates itself into a social, political and cultural environment that tends to be anti-establishment, its performance will be negatively influenced by this hostility.

In the long term, and from a more global viewpoint that takes account of political and social realities, the legitimacy, success and survival of firms may increasingly depend on the adoption of responsible behaviour with regard to the important problems of our era. Responsible firms have become conscious of the fact that their economic performance will not be sustainable if the environment deteriorates, or if social, political and intellectual forces become hostile to them.

By proactively assuming new responsibilities, firms encourage and accelerate the transformation of the development model. They also act with a long-term view and the will to integrate economic progress with the general interest and a more global common good.

They do not completely subordinate their sense of responsibility to the creation of immediate competitive advantages, as some American specialists in the strategy of the firm suggest (for example Porter, 2003). They act to transform the system and emerge from the single thought, and therefore take a series of gambles:

- In respect of strategy, their long-term competitive advantages will be based as much on social criteria as on quality and price; the citizen/consumer movement is going in this direction and will exert growing pressure on firms.
- Research and innovation will allow them to maintain or renew these competitive advantages by adapting existing products and services to the expectations of society, or by developing new products in response to these expectations.
- Motivating employees will increasingly depend on a coherence between work and the values of the citizen; people will think more about the nature of their work and its outcome; they will expect this important part of their life to have a meaning.
- In order to attract the key resources needed for sustainable development, firms will have to create a culture and an image that correspond to the expectations of society. This also applies to the recruitment of high-quality staff, as everyone knows that 'it is people that make the difference' (Lecerf, 1991). It might also be true for financial resources if ethical funds continue to develop, as well as for the public and political goodwill required for a favourable environment.

For companies taking more corporate social responsibility today is still a bet because unless a reformed development model is accepted and widely adopted the current model and its instrumental logic will remain dominant. The most enlightened firms can play a key role by promoting a transformation of the model, but by themselves they will not be able to extend this to the whole of the globalizing economy. So while their contribution will certainly be useful it will not be sufficient to transform the model. As we shall see, this effort will have to be part of a more general movement.

Voluntary or imposed change?

There are two conflicting views with regard to change. On the one hand the majority of companies believe that a voluntary change, initiated and conducted by them, will be sufficient to correct the deviations and defects of an unsatisfactory development model. On the other hand unions, antiglobalization militants and certain political parties advocate a transformation imposed by the law, government policies and the public authorities. We believe that it will be necessary to combine these two approaches in the framework of the new consultations discussed in the previous chapter.

Voluntary change has often been sparked by external pressure. Business leaders and managers are used to perceiving and understanding signals from the marketplace. When Shell's sales dipped in Germany during its dispute with Greenpeace over the sinking of the Brent Spar oil platform, the firm quickly understood the threat on its legitimacy. When consumers begin to boycott products for ethical or safety reasons the message spreads rapidly. The majority of firms want a favourable business environment, so when it becomes hostile they react promptly and often with vigour. The majority of the large companies selected as targets by NGOs have adapted their behaviour and improved their transparency, including Nike, Levi, Monsanto and Nestlé.

As we have seen, there are also enlightened executives who do not wait for a crisis or open conflict. They have a longer-term vision and understand that they must integrate the challenges of the future into their strategies. This is of course true of those who participate in the movement for social responsibility.

As far as their motives are concerned, there is no reason to question the sincerity of announcements of change, especially when they are accompanied by concrete transformations such as those described earlier.

One may regret the fact that it often takes external pressure or a scandal to bring about change, but this is the way with human affairs and what is important is that things are now moving and the system is evolving. One can always accuse business people of not being sincere and indulging in public relations without changing their behaviour, but when the pressures are sufficiently strong, or the challenges clearly perceived, attitudes do begin to change.

There is no guarantee that the new sense of responsibility will survive a lengthy economic crisis or the pressure of heightened competition. A legislative approach is called for if we wish to ensure the implementation of a sustainable development model and not rely on the hazards of circumstance or the goodwill of business leaders.

Even restricting ourselves to the specific function of the firm – i.e. economic progress – we must recognize that it may produce consequences that cannot be left to the private sector, either because they are beyond its scope or because the impact they have on society is such that they should depend on public action.

Such is the case with the negative aspects and consequences of the current system: damage to the environment, the growing power of the technosciences, the excessive influence of the financial markets, domination, exclusion and destructuring. These problems largely lie outside the scope of self-regulation by the firm or the market. They require intervention by the authorities and transformation of the development model.

Leaving the evolution towards this new model to the initiative of companies alone would amount to abandoning the political choice of priorities and the pace of change to the private sector alone. This goes against the more democratic and concerted approach suggested earlier.

The sincerity of responsible companies can be judged by the extent and speed of the changes they are prepared to accept, not only in their culture but also in the transformation of the development model. The most enlightened business leaders recognize the necessity of public intervention, in contrast to those who call for less state control, more liberalization and greater deregulation. State intervention obviously cannot be restricted to making the competitive game run more smoothly or controlling the accuracy of accounts and the honesty of managers, as the recent Sarbanes–Oxley law in the US sets out to do. It must also, and above all, guide the progress of companies and the market economy towards a more sustainable development model and the new responsibilities that implies. In several cases, public intervention will have to be international, either at the European or at the world level.

Such intervention will be tricky to design and implement. If it is too overpowering it will risk damaging the fragile mechanisms of creativity and arresting the dynamism of companies. If it is too timid or limited it will have insufficient influence on the economic system to make it abandon its instrumental logic and take up a broader purpose. A balance has to be found and this will depend on the art of governing. 'A process should be set in motion to make the rule of law prevail. One way is to make multinationals accountable to their countries of origin for infringements in any other country, with regards to three sets of norms: basic human rights, core labour standards (i.e. non minimum wages) and relevant multilateral environmental agreements' (Defraigne, 2004).

We can quote the example of the new regulation the European Commission wishes to impose on the chemical industry. Under the regulation the latter will be required to provide data proving the harmlessness of at least 30 000 chemical substances that hitherto have not been subject to any control. The governments of the three largest EU countries believe that such a measure could endanger the competitiveness of the European chemical industry. The Federation of German Industries maintains that the measure could destroy 1.7 million jobs in Germany alone. The Commission itself recognizes that the regulation could be difficult to implement and would cost European companies up to €32 billion.

More generally, and when there is no major stake, it would be more effective to set the directions to be pursued, the goals to be achieved, the boundaries that must not be crossed and what is clearly banned, rather than impose procedures and tools for action that apply to all companies, irrespective of size, sector or economic and technical developments.

Firms are capable of adapting and innovating in social matters and their creativity can be greater than that of the authorities. Concrete transformations depend more on the dynamism of entrepreneurs, the imagination of researchers and the ability to react quickly to opportunities and threats, than on laws, directives or regulations. The latter must therefore leave the field sufficiently open to allow the initiative of companies to develop.

The law can only control and it is no substitute for action or innovation. Economic progress is not decreed by law any more than employment or scientific discovery are. This is also true of social responsibility. Pernickety legislation must not prevent the most committed companies from going beyond what the law lays down. This view is held unanimously by the most enlightened executives. Control and direction – yes. Detailed rules and a one-size-fits-all approach – no.

This point of view has also been adopted by the European Commission. Following pressure from the unions and NGOs, its green book on the new social responsibilities of firms recommended that certain practices be made compulsory, such as maintaining a triple balance sheet and introducing ethical codes. In response the leaders of Corporate Social Responsibility Europe pointed out that situations varied markedly from sector to sector and company to company, and that norms that were too rigid would be less effective than voluntary measures, which in some cases were already further advanced than those proposed. They added that they were ready to go further than the law and discuss these 'best practices' with their peers in order to examine the possibility of putting them into general use. This approach prevailed and was incorporated into the definitive version of the green book (the *White Book on Governance*, European Commission, 2001).

A similar situation occurred in the US. A year after the passage of the Sarbanes–Oxley law, the Securities and Exchange Commission decided that in future accounting standards would be defined in terms of principles rather than rules.

As far as change is concerned, what is important is to initiate a process of transformation rather than proposing a one-size-fits-all blue print. This process will tend to organise the active participation of the main actors and orient them towards a shared vision of a development model. The concept of sustainable development offers a vision of this type and includes companies in the process.

From this point of view, one can suggest that the adoption by firms of social responsibility is a necessary but not sufficient condition to produce the desired results. A key part can be played by *avant-garde* movements such as Corporate Social Responsibility, provided they subscribe to a political and legal framework that can support and direct them. This is where the transformation of the firm meets the transformation of the development model.

10
Towards Sustainable Development?

Do not forget the future.

(Jewish proverb)

A new concept

Sustainable development is without doubt the concept that most faithfully translates at the general level the themes developed in this book: broadening the purpose of economic progress, the creation of a political and ethical culture, and mastery of the process of collective change.

A well-known definition can be found in the Brundtland Report (United Nations, 1989): 'Sustainable development is a development that responds to the needs of the present without compromising the capacity for future generations to respond to theirs.' This report marked the moment of recognition that the development model had to be rethought.

It was the start of a global process of reflection and action, in which public and private players were invited to confer on strategies for progress that would no longer be driven by the single thought and the narrow market ideology. In their book on the responsible firm, Alain Chaveau and Jean-Jacques Rosé (2003) describe the boldness and political capacity of those who launched the process and facilitated the 'emergence of the planetary awareness' that the Club of Rome had contributed towards. As these authors point out, sustainable development depends on the addressing of

177

two priority areas, in particular the essential needs of the most impoverished' and 'the limitations that the state of our techniques and of our social organization imposes on the capacity of the environment to respond to current and future needs'.

Here we find our questions about the meaning of economic progress and the purpose of the firm. We also find the idea that launching the process was more important for development than noble theoretical proposals that, in the absence of concrete actions, risked becoming quickly fossilized.

Several stages of this process took place after the publication of the report on sustainable development. Among the most important were the Rio Conference in 1992 and the Johannesburg Conference in 2002.

At Rio the Conference of the United Nations for the Environment and Development (CUNED) brought together

> NGOs, business leaders, high-level civil servants, a thousand ministers, ten thousand government delegates. It was a great 'fair' and a lot of work for preparing this first Earth summit; 178 countries adopted a set of mixed documents that established sustainable development as a basic principle and an unavoidable reference, that was reiterated at all the international conferences organized since then by the United Nations. (Chaveau and Rosé, 2003)

From this emerged Agenda 21, the agenda for the twenty-first century. This comprised a series of concrete recommendations that were subsequently taken up by firms that wished their activities to be more responsible in nature. The Brundtland Report and the Rio Conference created the framework for political action, into which these firms could integrate.

The year '1992 saw the birth of the World Business Council for Sustainable Development, an organization that has brought together 160 of the largest multinationals and that defines itself as a think-tank for sustainable development' (ibid.) This heralded the start of a connection between the economic strategies of firms and broader, more long-term political orientations. There was also an international affirmation of values capable of inspiring the ethics of the future, as well as a new vision of the purpose of economic progress.

The most enlightened firms, having found a new ethical and political perspective, understood that it offered the most suitable framework for responding to the deviations of a market economy that was poorly regulated at the international level and of growth with no clear purpose, as well as working to correct the complexity, limits and paradoxes of the current system.

The many firms that participated in the Johannesburg Conference spoke of their first achievements in the area of sustainable development. They expressed their willingness to take part in this global process and to enter into world-wide political consultation. In this they were responding to the invitation of the UN secretary general, Kofi Annan, who was convinced that sustainable development could not be achieved without the cooperation of the main economic players.

To this end Annan launched the Global Compact programme, under which the participating firms commit themselves to a new development model. The programme is based on principles that provide a concrete basis for the broadened aims and purpose and the new ethical and political culture of the responsible firm:

- Human rights: firms commit themselves to supporting human rights and respecting them in their sphere of influence, as well as ensuring that they are not implicated in violations of these rights.
- Work: these should be freedom of association and negotiation, abandonment of all forms of forced labour and child labour, and elimination of discrimination in recruitment and the workplace.
- The environment: firms commit themselves to supporting the principle of prudence in the face of environmental dangers and challenges, promoting a more responsible attitude and encouraging the development and distribution of technologies that do not damage the environment.

Our aim is not to discuss these principles but to stress their relevance for the cultural evolution of the firm. Their application will require courage, and also moral and political judgement when responding to the very different situations in different countries. Moreover a culture based on an ethics for the future is essential to the advancement of the new development model.

The Global Compact is interesting in that it offers a global political orientation. Other initiatives of this type have been launched around the world. One example is the European Manifesto of Firms against Exclusion, which is aimed at encouraging integration into the labour market, improving professional training, preventing job cuts or making them less painful, promoting the creation of new jobs, and contributing to measures to help particularly vulnerable areas or groups of people. The manifesto was drawn up by a number of socially responsible firms with the help of the European Commission.

The Lisbon Group (1995) advocates world cooperation in four domains:

- Basic needs: water, housing, food.
- The Earth: environmental protection and sustainable development.
- Culture: tolerance and dialogue between cultures.
- Democracy: working towards a system of world governance.

The first two points particularly concern firms. The group's approach is not aimed at supplanting the market economy but at substituting for it in areas where it does not operate. It suggests that firms' capacity for action should be utilized to help causes that are not profitable in the short term.

Needless to say, in the face of these initiatives for change the propagators of the single thought and the defenders of national interests are making a stand. One only has to note the resistance of certain states to the implementation of Agenda 21 and the Kyoto Protocol, and their attitude towards the dismantling of customs barriers, protection clauses, and the protection of intellectual property rights.

It is clear that a change in lifestyle is necessary in the advanced countries. This will be a major political challenge and can only be achieved in a progressive and democratic way. Here again the resistance will be very strong. The words used by President George Bush at Rio speak volumes: 'The American way of life is not negotiable' (quoted in Chaveau & Rosé, 2003).

That said, the concept of sustainable development offers a vision of the future that can complete the actions of responsible firms. We know that a vision is a necessary precondition for any transformation process, and that when it is realistic and shared it has the virtue of turning people towards the future. It radically alters their focus and behaviour: 'drawn by the future' they bring to bear infinitely more creative imagination, energy and organizational dynamism.

The new model will only emerge and develop if the majority of firms adopt such a vision and align their strategies to the global collective effort, involving other social players and international governance.

Towards world governance

If the national and international authorities have insufficient political will, the efforts of the most enlightened firms risk being stifled by the pressure of competition, the inertia of the system and the weight of reality and special interests. It is the economic and technical model that must be changed. As we have seen, it must be extracted from the straitjacket of the single thought and put to the service of the global common good.

This topic lies well outside the scope of this chapter so we shall restrict ourselves to mentioning a few priorities that relate directly to firms or over which they may have some influence: the progressive introduction of world governance, the implementation of new rules of the game, and widespread adoption of a sustainable development model.

World governance is essential if we are to respond to the challenges of the world. The fight against poverty, disease, illiteracy and environmental destruction calls for international policies.

In the face of a globalization that is almost exclusively economic and financial in nature, are we condemned to be subjected to the laws of a new empire dominated by the market and investment funds? Or can we conceive of a political, social and cultural change that would restore the balance and ensure that the economy better served the general interest?

Shall we succeed in combining the dynamism and creativity of the current model with correction of its deviations and the addressing of major challenges with which the market cannot or should not concern itself? We must equip ourselves with the political means of managing the paradoxes of a globalized world and the dangers that threaten it.

It is not a question of creating a centralized world government, but of the progressive implementation of new forms of international governance, called for by the size of the challenges, the complexity of the problems and the growing interdependence of the situations.

For the first time in history it is becoming necessary to manage systematically at the global level the problems of a human society that by 2050 is likely to consist of nine billion people. Clear and ambitious development objectives have been set by the UN for the first 15 years of the twenty-first century:

- Reduce by 50 per cent the number of people (currently about a billion) who do not have access to drinking water or live on less than one dollar per day.
- Provide primary education to all children in the world.
- Halt then reverse the spread of the world's most dangerous diseases, such as AIDS, malaria and tuberculosis.

Could we achieve the above without new forms of governance? The global common good requires that we invent new ways of defining and implementing it. How can we connect the different stages of political decision making? What networks and structures must be created? What methods of consultation, cooperation and democratic participation in the different levels of decision making and action are needed? Will the future of international relations not lie in managing interdependence through a set of networks (de Schoutheete, 2000)? The large economic players will obviously participate in some of these.

Thierry de Montbrial, a specialist in geopolitical evolution, writes of governance as follows:

> The idea of government as the organization in exclusive charge of public affairs at the heart of a state appears increasingly unsuitable. This is because the growth and complexity of interdependence largely deprive the word 'direction' of its normal meaning. But also because of the growing appropriation of public interest by society, a phenomenon that is tending – albeit slowly – to spread throughout the planet, despite some pockets of resistance.... The concept of governance, just like the regulation of complex networks of every kind (the question is currently the same for the internet), refers in a necessarily vague way to all the mechanisms of regulation at work in human systems (firms and other organizations, states,

groups of states . . .) that are not connected to a central decision-making unit but cause *ad hoc* coordination arrangements to intervene and are infinitely variable in both time and space. As a principle of organization, governance is opposed to the idea of hierarchy. One can associate with it the idea of subsidiarity. (de Montbrial, 2000)

It is by participating in networks that the firm will exercise its social responsibilities. It is by contributing to their creation and their effectiveness that it will encourage the emergence of the sustainable development model. Instead of fighting, through defensive lobbying, against the new forms of governance and the regulations required for sustainable development, it will participate in their formulation.

Those who speak of governance, of course, speak of debates and clashes of points of view. Responsible firms are beginning to participate in these debates. They are contributing their views and skills and are beginning to listen to opinions that differ from their own.

Governance also implies a degree of common action. To the mechanisms of competition will be added acts of cooperation that will make the know-how and strategic capacity of firms available to address the problems of the world (water, health, pollution and so on). One of the challenges in the renewal of governance at every level is probably to succeed in creating a fruitful multiplayer cooperation.

One of the priority actions will be to create governance bodies (institutions or networks) that can connect tasks of global interest with local policies and entrepreneurial skills.

With regard to *new rules of the game*, if we want to make the creativity of firms available to promote sustainable development the conditions for competition must be made more equal. To date competition policies have been aimed at making the markets function and preventing anything that might impair their effectiveness, such as trade arrangements, monopoly positions and even public intervention in the form of support, guarantees or the propping up of unsuccessful firms.

Future competition policies must include provisions for sustainable development in the areas of the environment, respect for human rights, the principle of precaution and so on. This is what the Global

Compact aims to do through the voluntary commitment of firms. In the absence of such policies there is a danger that, in the race for technical progress, market share and profit maximization, the competitive pressures on the responsible firm will reach the point of shattering its social strategies.

There have been cases of ethical, social or environmental dumping. Without a correlation between the performance of the firm and its new responsibilities, it appears that there is nothing to prevent this type of dumping from becoming a competitive weapon and causing the most enlightened firms to abandon their social commitment. In other words, if social dumping remains possible the internal logic of the current economic model might be sufficiently powerful to block the movement for responsibility and restore the established order of the single thought and a hard-line market logic.

This can only be avoided if the sustainable development model is widely adopted and gradually replaces the current model.

Widespread adoption of the sustainable development model cannot be achieved without resolute political intervention. Far from opposing this such intervention, responsible firms will support it and deploy their skills, creativity and capacity for action.

International political action will doubtless be the most difficult condition to fulfil, as well as the slowest and most fought over. Resistance will be widespread: defence of national interests by large countries, corruption among political leaders, industrial lobbies protecting their sectoral interests, indifference or egoistic posturing by advanced countries, and ethnic conflict and fundamentalism fed by humiliation, lack of prospects and despair.

Nevertheless if we are to reduce poverty, combat disease and protect the planet we must have political action that is sufficiently strong and global to overcome individual, sectoral and national interests. This can only be done through consultation and persuasion. This is the aim of the UN initiatives in this domain. It is important to strengthen and reorient the existing international institutions, but failing strong support from states there is a danger of acting too slowly to avoid new catastrophes.

In order to humanize globalization it will be necessary to regulate the world economy by means of treaties and international agreements. A greater financial contribution by the rich countries (probably through taxation) should eventually be obtained to fight extreme poverty and provide the poorest countries with means and resources for their development. But all this must be done sensitively, at the right time, with sufficient consensus among the players and without paralyzing the mechanisms of innovation and creativity.

If market mechanisms can be used to influence or focus the decisions of firms or consumers they will bring important gains in effectiveness and time. The Kyoto Protocol 'is the first international treaty on the environment to attempt to harness market mechanisms, in which emission credits can be traded, to achieve its goals in the most cost-effective way possible (Houlder, 2004). In the area of clean energy sources, 'the establishment of market-based mechanisms to cap and trade greenhouse gas emissions will create space in the market for a new set of energy sources by making emissions more expensive... Such a system would prompt business to use its knowledge of technology, markets and consumer preferences to transform possibilities into reality' (Browne, 2004).

Innovation and creativity play in the same direction. This is the case for instance of micro-credits launched by the Gramin Bank. Using entrepreurship better to adapt products and services to the needs of poor people might bring a significant contribution to initiate market mechanisms in developing countries (Prahalad, 2004). Moreover, if we want really to help the poor countries to fight their extreme poverty and to 'take-off' economically, we will have greatly to increase our contribution not only in terms of financing but by providing them with key material and immaterial resources of economic development.

To enable the sustainable development model to advance, it is important for the EU countries to speak with one voice. The EU has become a prime economic and commercial power in the world and offers an appropriate space for dialogue. Its democratic institutions and political parties are involving themselves in the preparation of a blueprint for a sustainable future. The EU strategy for sustainable development, approved at Gothenburg in 2001, constitutes a major step in this direction. The problem is to extend this to the global level. As the EU has successfully handled its difficult integration it ought to be able to put together a development model that suits the needs of the present and is likely to attract the support of other regions of the world.

Will the pressure of public opinion, society, and the most enlightened economic and political players be sufficient? This is a challenging question for those who wish to commit themselves to becoming responsible.

The aim of this book has not been to suggest details of a new development model but to underline the importance of one for firms that see themselves as responsible. The moves made by the most enlightened of them are in line with such a model and are contributing to its achievement. These firms are changing their culture, committing themselves to European and world-wide consultation, and working to convince their peers to adopt this vision of the future. They are beginning to recognize the need for new regulations aimed at combining economic progress with the general interest, which has become more complex and more global. Instead of resisting these regulations by defensive lobbying, they are participating in drawing them up.

By themselves, firms cannot change the present system, but by integrating their actions into the international movement for sustainable development they are playing a decisive part in bringing it about. They are focusing their extraordinary power of action on a global common good.

Creative enterprise, Prometheus, will be more explicitly at the service of human progress.

Postscript

As Paul Valéry has said, reaching a conclusion is stupid. We shall not offer any conclusions here because the debate is ongoing and the process of transformation has scarcely begun. Rather we shall limit ourselves to three final remarks as a reminder of the urgency of the necessary changes, the possibility of taking a reformist path and the importance of good leadership if the transformation is to succeed.

Urgency is required because the current development model is unsustainable.

The risks in the medium to long term are clear: the continuing rise of a system that has no clear purpose; failure to alleviate world poverty, despair, insecurity and chaos; the pollution of the planet, overexploitation of its resources and reduction of biological diversity; and the bad use of science.

In the short term excessive regulation at the national level and the lack of coordinated regulation at the global level is threatening the entrepreneurial dynamism and economic creativity that are so necessary for sustainable development.

Shall we be able to move quickly enough to transform our development model in such a way as to reduce the threats that weigh on the planet, or will we allow ourselves to be carried along by the negative deviations of the current system?

In the face of a risk we can react in only one of two ways: we can attempt to reduce the probability of it occurring, or we can try to minimize its impact after it has become a reality. The urgency forced upon us by the speed, complexity and uncertainty of the matters described in this book do not permit any delay – we must act before it is too late. 'There is nothing in the world that does not have its decisive moment and the masterpiece of good conduct is see and seize this moment' (Retz).

A proactive stand by responsible firms would help to reduce the major defects of the current system: let us hope that such a stand becomes widespread.

Will the transformation of the development model take place through *reforms* or through more revolutionary methods?

In the West there is a tendency to favour evolution over revolution. Recent historical events have taught us that revolutionary change has an enormous cost in terms of human suffering and the destruction of resources, organizations and the very impulses of dynamism and creativity. Few NGOs take a revolutionary approach. The West no longer seems to believe in this method of change.

And yet if one looks at things from a world perspective, is not a revolution possible? Are not injustice, humiliation, poverty, economic domination, public powerlessness, despair and fanaticism sufficient to unleash widespread violence and chaos? Are not the current terrorist actions an early warning sign of the radical upheaval that we call revolution?

It is the time available to improve society that separates evolution from revolution. Peaceful transformation is possible if it is embarked upon early enough to encourage support, hope and a belief in better times.

If we allow major problems to fester in the belief that if we wait they will sort themselves out, rather than intervening to resolve them, the process of change may well take a radical turn. This was clearly the case with the *Ancien Régime* in France, which was slow to introduce the required political and fiscal reforms. It was also the case with the Catholic Church during the Reformation, when it lost its unity by refusing to listen to appeals from below, correct abuses and change with the times. It was also the case with the Russian Tsars, who were unable to alter their social and political system despite spectacular economic development.

Our capacity and will to transform our development model will govern its future performance, if not its survival. Will the reforms that we are embarking upon be sufficiently far-reaching? Will we succeed in achieving them in time? This will depend of the perceptiveness of our governments and the people who have elected them.

It will also depend on firms. Their move towards greater responsibility will certainly not be enough to resolve all the problems of the world, but they will be able to make a powerful contribution in the central sphere of economic development, where they play the leading role.

This is where political and moral commitment is essential. This is where the social dimension of the firm finds its meaning.

Finally, *good leadership is required at every level*. We have enough managers, technicians and financiers. What is still needed for a true transformation to occur is a sufficient number of leaders who are capable of bringing it about by inspiring and motivating those who must implement the necessary measures.

Whereas Frederick Taylor (1965) recommended replacing the government of men with the administration of things, almost the opposite has to be done today. Economics and politics must be rebalanced.

If we define management narrowly, we can say that it is above all the administration of things: objectives, budgets, strategic analyses, plans, methods, procedures. Leadership is the art of motivating, communicating, empowering, and convincing people to accept change.

Leadership is based on moral authority, which is one of the most difficult realities to understand. All that research has come up with is this first truth: the foundation of leaders' authority over those they lead lies not only in their ability to direct or govern, but also, and perhaps above all, in those who are directed and governed and who accept or refuse to follow them.

If they persistently say 'no', the leaders' authority disappears. They can keep their power but they will have no authority. Power is the ability to constrain, authority is the ability to convince. It stems from the moral order, whereas power arises from the legal order or force.

Moral authority requires talent and character. All those who have engaged in action know that great leaders owe part of their authority to their personal qualities. This has been a constant fact throughout human history. The numerous works devoted to leadership agree on some essential virtues: a vision of the future that can be transformed into a common endeavour; attention to people and the ability to communicate with them, convince them, motivate them and inspire them; devotion to a common aim, a spirit of service and the absence of self-interest; character, courage and firmness; possession of values that are clearly proclaimed and visibly practised.

These are personalities of a different stature from those who are content to lock themselves into the single thought. We are speaking of those enlightened leaders who have been described so well by Joubert: 'heads where there is light, hearts that have movement, souls that have taste'. It is to these people that this book is dedicated.

Notes

Preface

1. Quotes are taken from Aeschylus, *Prometheus Bound*, from the French translation (*Prométhée enchaîné*) translated by André Bonnard, Lausanne, Mermoz, 1946.
2. The European Academy of Business in Society (EABIS). In 2003 the copresidents were Étienne Davignon of Suez and CSR-Europe, and Mads Ovlissen of Novo Nordisk.

1 The Creative Enterprise

1. Here the term *raison d'être* is used for the French word *finalité*. It means the ultimate end of action – what gives the action its moral and political justification and therefore its legitimacy. It throws light on the meaning of action. The closest word in English is 'purpose', and it will be used in this sense.
2. Aeschylus, *Prometheus Bound*, trans. G. M. Cookson, Encyclopaedia Britannica, Inc 1980.
3. It is significant that a dictionary definition of the enterprise includes the 'implementation of a project'. 'What we imagine, we can make happen', proclaims the US giant, General Electric.
4. Michaël Dell, quoted in Harvey (2003).
5. Interview with Nobuyuku Idei, President of Sony, *Financial Times*, 23 October 2003.
6. Also, 'make a killing', a 'risky weapon in the corporate armoury', 'fire power', 'smart bombs', and so on.

2 New Weapons: the Technosciences

1. Three per cent of GNP in the US and Japan, 1.9 per cent in Europe.
2. The first Ethernet system (1973) operated at 2.94 megabytes (about a paragraph per second); today it has reached 10 000 megabytes (10 gigabytes), and 100 000 megabytes per second is within reach.

3 New Spaces: Globalization of the Market Economy

1. International commerce increased from $380 billion in 1950 to $5860 billion in 1997 (*World Economic Outlook*, International Monetary Fund, October 1997).
2. *Harvard Business Review*, May 1983; Tomkins Financial Times, 6 May 2003.
3. The concept of 'slack' refers a certain 'give' in the system that prevents it from becoming paralyzed or resistant to change. Cf. Penrose (1959).

4. Gerald Levin, president of America Online, *Financial Times*, 7 February 2000.
5. Hilland Waters, AOL-Time Warner immerger, *Financial Times*, 11 January 2000.
6. European Aerospace and Defence Systems.
7. Interview with Steve Case, *Financial Times*, 25 February 2000.

4   New Power: Political Deficit and Ethical Vacuum

1. 'There is nothing wrong in doing what will benefit the whole of humanity... The pursuit of the American national interest will create the conditions that will promote freedom, the markets and peace' (Condoleezza Rice, *Foreign Affairs*, January/February 2000).
2. Private military firms in the US provide logistical support in the armed struggle against drug trafficking in Colombia, and assist peace keeping in some countries.
3. M. Allais, winner of the Nobel Prize for economics in 1988.
4. Cato Institute pamphlet, 2000, quoted by Simon London in 'Corporate governance', *Financial Times*, 20 August 2002.
5. Egil Bodd, quoted in Dyer (2002).
6. Overell (2002), commenting on *The Representation of Business in English Literature*, Reading 53, Institute of Economic Affairs, December 2000.
7. The European Round Table of industrialists consists of a group of about 50 heads of Europe's most internationally successful firms.
8. Here we shall restrict ourselves to matters that involve firms. We shall not tackle fundamental political areas such as security, the maintenance of peace, the control of weapons of mass destruction and so on that also reveal the powerlessness of states and call for world governance.
9. The *Prestige* sank on 19 November 2002 off the Spanish coast.
10. As pointed out by E. Davignon, copresident of the EU–Japan Business Dialogue Round Table, 'We need a protocol, it is essential. If we wait, there will be negative economic effects. But it is clear that if the USA does not play a role, the objectives of Kyoto will not be achieved' (*Financial Times*, 11 July 2000).
11. In the sense used by J. K. Galbraith in *American Capitalism* (1956).
12. At the UN and EU level.

5   An Unsustainable System?

1. In particular the movement associated with the social responsibilities of the firm – see Part II.
2. Brother Samuel Rouvillois, conference in Saint-Nom-la-Bretêche, 1998.
3. In the UK the 180 000 cases of mad cow disease, or BSE, led to the slaughter of 4.3 million cattle. The final cost of this insanity was €5.6 billion.
4. For example, in developing countries between 1970 and 1997 life expectancy rose from 55 years to 65, infant mortality fell from 107 to 58.9 per 1000, and the level of illiteracy fell from 45 per cent in 1980 to 30 per cent in 1995.

5. 'In terms of box office takings, the films produced by the major American producers – Hollywood – add up to a share of 85% of the world market. Of the 20 highest world box-office takings in 2000, 19 films were from the major Hollywood studios and US–British coproductions' (Paris, 2003).

6. The sum paid for exclusive distribution rights to the British football Premier League by British Sky Broadcasting (BSkyB – satellite TV) amounted to €1.46 billion.

7. See especially Roche (1998) and Martou, (2002).

8. These assertions are perhaps rather overstated. In advanced countries there are incidences of competitive domination, but they are rare and never last long.

9. This section draws on Lisbon Group (1995) and Fontela (1998).

10. In ancient Greece Aristophanes, disturbed by the corruption and decay that reigned in Athens, asked if anyone knew where he could buy a nose without holes.

11. In 2002, 4.9 million people died from smoking-related diseases, and the WHO has warned that, in the absence of coordinated regulation, this figure could reach 10 million by 2020.

12. Warren Buffet, letter in 2000 to Berkshire Hathaway shareholders.

13. The following discussion draws heavily on case studies published in the *Financial Times* in 2001 and 2002.

14. See especially the *Financial Times* and *Le Monde*, 3 July 2002.

15. 'This divine sense of proportion which is modesty' (Morand, P., 1992).

7 The Ethics of the Future

1. See especially the International Council for Science, which involves more than 100 academics. Its report (2004) on GMOs explains what is known and what is not known, as well as points of agreement and disagreement among 50 research groups around the world.

9 The Move Towards Social Responsibility

1. H. C. de Bettignies, comments made at his retirement ceremony, held by INSEAD on 19 November 2003.

2. N. Mintzberg, interview in *Financial Times*, 16 September 2003; see also Mintzberg (1973).

3. EABIS Survey of Teaching and Research in Europe, Brussels, 2003.

4. This passage draws on de Brabandère *et al.* (2000).

Bibliography

Aeschyllus (1946) *Prométhée enchaîné* (translated by Bonnard, A., Genève: Mermod).

Albert, M. (1991) *Capitalisme contre capitalisme* (Paris: Seuil).

Albert, M. (2002) 'Quel modèle d'entreprise pour un développement durable?', Communication à l'Académie des Sciences morales et politiques, Paris, December.

Allais, M. (2002) 'La crise intellectuelle du monde occidental. Désagrégation morale,' *Le Figaro*, 19–20 October.

Aristophane (1965) *La Paix* (trans. de V. H. Debidour) (Paris: Gallimard).

Aristote (1986) *Politique* (Paris: Belles Lettres).

Arnsperger, Ch. and Van Parijs, Ph. (2000) *Ethique economique et Sociale* (Paris: La Découverte et Syros).

Aron, R. (1983) *Mémoires* (Paris: Julliard).

Auerbach, A. (ed.) (1989) *Corporate Takeovers* (Chicago, Ill.: University of Chicago Press).

Augustine, Saint, (1959) *La Cité de Dieu* (Tournai: Desclée de Brouwer).

Bangemann, M. (1994) *Europe and the Global Information Society* (Brussels: European Commission).

Barber, T. and Benoit, B. (2002) The Mannesmann affair, *Financial Times*, 26 July.

Baumol, W. J. (2002) *The Free Market Innovation Machine* (Princeton, NJ: Princeton University Press).

Beck, U. and Giddens, A. (1994) *Reflexive modernization* (New York: Stanford University Press and Polity Press).

Belot, J. (2002) Editorial, *Le Figaro*, 2 July.

Bergson, H. (1932) *Les deux sources de la morale et de la religion* (Paris: Presses Universitaires de France).

Berle, A. A. and Means, G. (1959) *The Modern Corporation and Private Property* (New York: Harcourt).

Bernis, Cardinal de (1980) Mémoires (Paris: Mercure de France).

Berten, I. and Lavigne J. C. (2003) *Mondialisation et universalisme. Echos bibliques* (Brussels: Lumen Vitae).

Betts, P. (2002) Risk and Reward, *Financial Times*, 16–17 February.

Braudel, F. (1979) *Civilisation matérielle, économie et capitalisme* (Paris: Armand Colin).

Browne, J. (2004) 'Small Steps to Limit Climate Change' *Financial Times*, 30 June.

Brown-Humes, G. (2002) 'Pinstripe plunder' puts senior banker in line of fire, *Financial Times*, 16/17 February.

Brown-Humes, G. and Hall, W. (2002) Investors force Barnevik out over pension, *Financial Times*, 14 February.

Buckley, N. (2003) Government vs Industry: 50 years of Fraud, *Financial Times*, 8 August.

Buffet, Warren (2000) letter to Berkshire Hattaway Shareholders.

Cadbury, A. (1992) *Corporate Governance: A Framework for Implementation* (London: Blackwell).

Calame, P. (2001) *Refonder la gouvernance mondiale pour répondre aux defis du 21ème siècle* (Paris: L'Alliance pour un monde responsable).

Calame, P. and Talmant, A. (1997) *L'Etat au cœur* (Paris: Desclée de Brouwer).

Castells, E. (1998) *La société en réseaux, l'ère de l'information* (Paris: Fayard).

Centre européen du civisme (2003) *L'entreprise surveillée* (Brussels: Bruylant).

Chaffin, J. and Fidler, S. (2002) 'Enron revealed to be rotten to the core', *Financial Times*, 9 April.

Chamfort, S. (1960) *Œuvres* (Paris: J. J. Pauvert).

Chaveau, A. and Rosé, J. J. (2003) *L'entreprise responsable* (Paris: Editions d'organisation).

Cheng, I. and Hill, A. (2003) 'The Barons of Bankruptcy', *Financial Times*, 31 July, 1 and 2 August.

Cicéro (1962) *13ième Philippique* (trans. A. Boulanger) (Paris: Les Belles Lettres).

Cobbaut, R. (1997) 'Ethique et régulation des systèmes financiers', in *cours d'Ethique des affaires et finalité de l'entreprise* (Louvain: IAG, Université de Louvain).

Cobbaut, R. and Lenoble, J. (eds) (2003) *Corporate Governance, an Institutionalist Approach*, The Hague, London and New York: Kluwer Law International).

Coleridge, N. (1993) *Paper Tigers*, (London: Heinemann).

Collins, J. and Porras, J. (1994) *Built to Last: Successful Habits of Visionary Companies* (New York: HarperCollins).

Collomb, B. (2002a) 'Entreprise, humanisme et mondialisation', in Th. de Montbrial (ed.), *La France du nouveau siècle* (Paris: Presses Universitaires de France).

Collomb, B. (2002b) *Introduction to Building a Sustainable World, A first Report on our Economic, Social and Environmental Performance* (Paris: Lafarge).

Crivallero, R. (2002) 'L'impunité des "poubelles des mers" ', *La Libre Belgique*, 20 November.

Crozier, M. and Friedberg, E. (1977) *L'acteur et le système* (Paris: Seuil).

Daimler Chrysler (2002) *Portrait of a World Corporation* (Stuttgart: Daimler Chrysler).

Davignon, E. (2002) EABIS First Colloquium, INSEAD, Fontainebleau, 5–6 July.

Davignon, E. (2003) 'A European Campaign for Sustainable Growth and Human Progress', *European Business Forum*, no. 18 (Winter).

de Bernis, F. (1980) *Mémoires* (Paris: Mercure de France).

de Bettignies, H. C. (2002) Speech presented to the First Colloquium of the European Academy for Business in Society, (Fontainebleau, 5–6 July) June.

de Brabandère, L. (1998) *Le management des idées: de la créativité à l'innovation* (Paris: Dunod).

de Brabandère, L., Besnier, J. M. and Handy, C. (2000) *Erasme, Machiavel, More. Trois philosophes pour les managers d'aujourd'hui* (Paris: Village Mondial).

de Brabandère, L. (2004) *Le Sens des ideès* (Paris: Dunod).

de Duve, Ch. (2002) *A l'écoute du vivant* (Paris: Odile Jacob).

Defraigne, P. (2004) Creating a level playing field for CSR, in *Corporate Social Responsibility*, A Special Report, (London: EBF European Business Forum) Summer 2004.

de Jonquières, G. (2003a) 'Battles among regulators could damage trade', *Financial Times*, 26 May.

de Jonquière, G. (2003b) 'Comment and Analysis', *Financial Times*, 14 May.

de Jonquière, G., Alden, Buck, T. (2003b) Comments and analysis on genetically modified crops, *Financial Times*, 14 May.

de Keuleneer, E. (2003) *Aspects éthiques de la surveillance des entreprises par le marché et les fusions et acquisitions in L'entreprise surveillée* (Brussels: Bruylant).

Delcourt, J. and de Woot, Ph. (2000) *Les défis de la globalisation: Babel ou Pentecôte?* (Louvain-la-Neuve: Presses Universitaires de Louvain).

de Montbrial, Th. (2000) *Le Monde au tournant du siècle* (Paris: Dunod).

de Montbrial, Th. (2002) *La France au tournant du siècle* (Paris: Presses Universitaires de France).

de Romilly, J. (1992) *Pourquoi la Grèce?* (Paris: Editions de Fallois).

de Schoutheete, Ph. (2000) 'Europe in the 21st Century', communication presented to the Colloquium of Yalta, 8 May.

de Tocqueville, A. (1952) *L'Ancien régime et la révolution* (Paris: Gallimard).

de Woot, Ph. (1962) *La fonction d'entreprise* (Louvain: Nauwelaerts).

de Woot, Ph. (1990) *High Technology Europe: Strategic Issues for Global Competitiveness* (Oxford: Blackwell).

de Woot, Ph. (1998) *Méditation sur le pouvoir* (Paris and Brussels: de Boeck Université).

de Woot, Ph. and Desclée, X. (1984) *Le management stratégique des groupes européens* (Paris: Economica).

de Woot, Ph. and Winterscheid, B. C. (1997) 'The evolution of strategic vision and capability in Lafarge' in A. Sinatra (ed.), *Corporate Transformation* (Norwell and Dordrecht: Kluwer).

Dron, D. (2000) 'Environment: les enjeux du prochain siècle', in Montbrial, Th. and Jacquet, P., *Ramsès 2001* (Paris: Dunod).

Dupriez, L. (1949) *Des mouvements économiques généraux* (Louvain: Nauwelaerts).

Dupriez, L. (1959) *Philosophie des conjonctures économiques* (Louvain: Nauwelaerts).

Dyer, G. (2002) 'Europe seeks pill to calm fears over US style drug advertising', *Financial Times*, 23 October.

Eigen, P. (2003) *Das Netz der Korruption* (Frankfurt: Campus Verlag).

Eliot, T. S. (1948) *The Rock* (London: Penguin Books).

Ellington, J. (1997) *Cannibals with Forks – The Triple Bottom Line of 21st Century Business* (Oxford: Capstone).

Ellsworth, R. R. (2002) *Leading with Purpose* (Stanford University Press).

Eschyle (1946) *Prométhée enchaîné* (trans. André Bonnard) (Geneva: Mermod) and trans. G. M. Cookson, Encyclopaedia Britannica, Inc 1980.

Euripides (1962) *Tragédies* (Paris: Gallimard).

European Academy of Business in Society (EABIS) (2003) *Survey of Teaching and Research in Europe on CSR* (Brussels: EABIS).

European Business Forum, *Special Reports on Corporate Social Responsibility* (London: 2003 and 2004).

European Commission (2001) *White Book on Governance* (Brussels: European Commission).

European Commission (2001) *Livre Vert: Promouvoir un cadre européen pour la responsabilité Sociale des entreprise* (Bruxelles: European Union).

European Commission (2002) *Une Contribution des entreprises an developpement durable* (Bruxells: CE).

European Round Table (ERT) and Conférence des recteurs européens (CRE) (1994) *Education for Europeans* (Brussels: ERT and CRE).

Feuerbach, L. (2001) *Manifeste philosophique*, textes choisis (Paris: Presses Universitaires de France).

Finkelstein, S. (2003) 'Why do smart executives fail?', *Financial Times*, 12 February.

Firn, D. (2003) 'GSK tops drug purchase league', *Financial Times*, 19 May.

Fitoussi, J.-P. (2003) 'Voie étroite ou voie large de l'économie politique?', paper presented at the Symposium on the 100th Anniversary of Leon-H. Dupriez, Louvain-la-Neuve, 14 November.

Fontela, E. (1998) 'The Era of Finance', *Futures*, vol. 30, no. 8, pp. 749–68.

Fourez, G. (1988) *La construction des sciences: introduction à la philosophie et à l'éthique des sciences* (Brussells: De Boeck).

Freeman, R. E. (1984) *Strategic Management: a Stakeholder Approach* (Boston: Pitman).

Friedberg, L. and Crozier, M. (1977) *L'acteur et le système* (Paris: Le Seuil).

Friedman, M. (1970) 'The Social Responsibility of Business is to Increase its Profits', *Time Magazine*, 13 September.

Fukuyama, F. (1992) *La fin de l'histoire et le dernier homme* (Paris: Flammarion).

Fusaro, P. C. and Miller, R. M. (2002) *What went wrong at Enron?* (New York: John Wiley).

Galbraith, J. K. (1956) *American Capitalism: The Concept of Countervailing Powers* (Boston, Mass.: Houghton).

Gattaz, Y. (2002) *La moyenne entreprise, championne de la croissance durable* (Paris: Fayard).

Gheshé, A. (1993) *Le Mal. Dieu pour penser* (Paris: Editions du Cerf).

Ghoshal, S. (2003) 'Business Schools share the blame for Enron', *Financial Times*, 18 July.

Glassman, J. (2003) Grasso's greed is not the issue for the NYSE, *Financial Times*, 16 September.

Goldsmith, E. and Mander, J. (eds) (2001) *Le procès de la mondialisation* (Paris: Fayard).

Gramsci, A. (1978) *Political Writings* (London: Lawrence and Wishhart Ltd).

Grousset, R. (1946) *Bilan de l'Histoire* (Paris: Plon).

Guillebaud, J. C. (1999) *La refondation du monde* (Paris: Seuil).

Guillebaud, J. C. (2001) *Le principe d'humanité* (Paris: Seuil).

Habermas, J. (1987) *Théorie de l'agir communicationnel* (Paris: Fayard).

Habermas, J. (1992) *De l'éthique de la discussion* (Paris: Editions du Cerf).

Harvey, F. (2003) 'Warriors wield new weapons from armoury', *Financial Times*, 6 August.

Havel, V. (1989) *Essais Politiques* (Paris: Calman-Levy).

Hertsgaard, M. (2002) *The Eagle's Shadow, why America Fascinates and Infuriates the World* (New York: Bloomsbury).

Holec, N. (1998) *Villes et développement durable* (Paris: Ministère de l'Equipement, Centre de documentation sur l'urbanisme).

Houlder, V. (2004) 'Environment. A change in the climate', *Financial Times*, 20 May.

Houtart, F. (2002) *Editorial d'Alternatives Sud*, vol. 10 (Paris: CETRI, L'Harmattan).

Houtart, F. and Amin Samir (eds) (2002) *Mondialisation des résistances. L'Etat des luttes 2002* (Paris: L'Harmattan).

Ide, P. (2003) 'Venez les essayer les nouvelles petites', *La Libre Belgique*, 22 May.

International Council for Science (2004) *Report on Genetically Modified Organism: MOC/Crops Defaults* (Paris: ICF).

Jacob, F. (1997) *La souris, la mouche et l'homme* (Paris: Editions Odile Jacob).

Jacquet, P. (2001) 'Petit bréviaire de la contestation', in Montbrial, Th., and Jacquet P., *Ramsès 2002* (Paris: Dunod).

Janssen, D. (2003) The Key to Corporate Longevity (*European Business Forum*). London.

Jenkins, P. (2002) Mannesmann Takeover, *Financial Times*, 15 January.

Jensen, M. and Meckling, W. (1976) 'Theory of the Firm: managerial behavior agency costs and ownership structure', *Journal of Finance Economics*, vol. 3.

Johnson, J. (2003) Saga enters unchartered legal waters, *Financial Times*, 12–13 July.

Jonas, H. (2000) *Le principe responsabilité* (Paris: Champs Flammarion).

Joubert, J. (1966) *Pensées* (Paris: Union Générale d'Editions).

Kant, E. (2004) La critique la raison pure (Paris: Presses Universitairs de France).

Kay, J. (2002) 'A vital item is missing', *Financial Times*, 29 January.

Kay, J. (2004) *Everlasting Light Bulbs* (Amsterdam: The Erasmus Press).

Kelleher, E. (2003) 'Heard the Gossip ?', *Financial Times*, 22 August.

Kingo, L. (2003) Speech at the second EABIS colloquium on CSR, Copenhagen, 19–20 September.

Kroll, D. (2002) 'Dupont's 200 years of integrity', *Financial Times*, 8 October.

Keynes, J. M. (1936) *General Theory of Employment, Interest and Money* (New York: Horcourt Brace).

Lacordaire, H. D. (1996) *Correspondance in Édite: 1830–1861*, Lacordaire, *Montalembert* (Paris: Cerf).

Ladrière, J. (2001) 'L'humanisme contemporain', in Quid, *Revista de Filosofia, Numero 1: Sobre a experiencia* (Lisbon: Livros Cotovia).

Lafarge (2002a) *Premier Rapport sur notre Performance économique, sociale et environnementale* (Paris: Lafarge).

Lafarge (2002b) *Deuxième rapport de développement durable* (Paris: Lafarge).

La Fontaine, J. de (1966) *Fables* (Paris: Garnier Flammarion).

Lambert, D. (1999) *Sciences et théologie* (Brussels: Lessius).

Lambin, J. J. and Chumpitaz, R. (2002) *Marketing stratégique et opérationnel: pour une gouvernance par le marché* (Paris: Dunod).

La Rochefoucauld (1964) *Maximes et Mémoires* (Paris: Union Générale d'Editions).

Latour, B. (1999) 'La modernité est terminée', in *Le progrès, une idée morte* (Paris: Le Monde, 29 August 1998).

Lecerf, O. (1991) *Au risque de gagner. Le métier de dirigeant* (Paris: Editions de Fallois).

Lemaître, F. (2002) 'Messier La Guigne', *Le Monde*, 3 July.

Levinas, E. (1972) *Humanisme de l'autre homme* (Montpellier: Fata Morgana).

Levitt, T. (1983) The Globalization of Markets, *Harvard Business Review*, May–June, vol. 61, no. 1.

Lippens, M. (2004) *Report on Corporate Governance* (Brussels, FEB).

Lippens, M. (2000) *Quelle identité pour l'entreprise sans frontières* (Brussels: paper presented at les Grandes Conférences Catholiques, 7 February 2000).

Lisbon Group (1995) *Limits to Competition* (Cambridge, Mass.: MIT Press).

London, S. (2002) 'Corporate Governance', *Financial Times*, 20 August.

London, S. (2003) 'Don't stop thinking about tomorrow', *Financial Times*, 4 August.

Lundberg, M. and Milanovic, B. (2000) 'The truth about global inequality' *Financial Times*, 25 October.

Lundberg, M. and Milanovic, B. (2003) The simultaneous evolution of growth and inequalities, *Economic Journal*, vol. 113, no. 48.

Lundberg, M. and Squire, L. (1999) *Report on Inequalities* (Washington, DC: World Bank).

Machiavelli, N. (1978) *Oeuvre Complètes* (Paris: Gallimard).

Maesschalk, M. (1995) 'L'éthique entre formalisme et subjectivité', in *Ethique des affaires et finalité de l'entreprise* (Louvain la Neuve: CIACO).

Malraux, A. (1972) *La tentation de l'Occident* (Paris: Grasset).

Margolin, J. C. (1967) *Erasme* (Paris: Seuil).

Martin, P. (2002) 'A return to public companies', *Financial Times*, 2 July.

Martin, P. and Gowers, A. (2001) 'Gates' Vision of the Future', *Financial Times*, 8 September.

Martou, F. (2002) 'L'eau, le bien commun et la gouvernance', paper (14 January) presented at the 2002 Annual World Social Forum, Porto Alegre.

Marx, K. (1848) *Le manifeste du parti communiste* (Brussels).

Michelet, J. (1974) *La Révolution francaise* (Paris: Jean de Bonnot).

Mirabeau, G. (1974) *Discours*, quoted in Michelet.

Mintzberg, N. (1973) *The Nature of Managerial Work* (New York: Harper and Row).

Moises, N. (2002) 'Tangled roots of corporate scandals', *Financial Times*, 30 September.

Molière (1965) *Oeuvres Complètes* (Paris: Gallimard).

Monks, A. G. (2003) *The New Global Investors* (Capstone).

Montesquieu, C.-L. (1987) *Considération sur les causes de la grandeur des Romains et de leur décadence* (Paris: Olivier Orban).

Morand, P. (1992) *Nouvelles Complètes* (Paris: Gallimard).

Morsing, M. and Thyssen, C. (eds) (2003) *Corporate Values and Responsibility. The Case of Denmark* (Copenhagen: Sanfundslitteratuur).

Moussé, J. (1989) *Fondements d'une éthique professionnelle* (Paris: Les éditions d'organisation).

Musil, R. (1961) *L'homme sans qualités* (Paris: Seuil).

Nakamoto, M. and Bort, T. (2003) 'Sony's Mission', *Financial Times*, 10 February.

Nonaka, I. and Hirotaka, T. (1995) *The Knowledge-Creating Company* (New York: Oxford University Press).

Novo Nordisk (2003a) *Annual Report 2002* (Copenhagen: Novo Nordisk).

Novo Nordisk (2003b) *Sustainability Report 2002* (Copenhagen: Novo Nordisk).

Orange, M. (2002) 'Jean-Marie Messier', *Le Monde*, 2 July.

Organisation des Nations-Unies (1989) *Notre avenir à tous* (Montreal: Les éditions du fleuve).

Overell, S. (2002) 'Forever the Villain of the Piece', *Financial Times*, 28 June.

Owen, D. (2000) 'Gravity stalks the balancing act at Vivendi', *Financial Times*, 14 July.

Paris, M. (2003) 'Industries culturelles et Mondialisation', in Montbrial Th. and Jacquet, P., *Ramsès 2003* (Paris: Dunod).

Peguy, Ch. (1912) *Clio* (Paris: Gallimard).

Penrose, E. (1959) *The Theory of the Growth of the Firm* (Oxford: Blackwell).

Petrella, R. (ed.) (1995) *Limits to competition* (Cambridge, Mass.: MIT Press).

Petrella, R. (1998) *Le manifeste de l'eau, pour un combat mondial* (Paris: Labor).

Porter, M. (2003) 'Corporate Social Responsibilities: The Role of Corporate Philanthropy', paper presented at the Second Colloquium of the European Academy of Business in Society, Copenhagen, 19–20 September.

Prahalad, C. K. (2004) *The Failure at the Bottom of the Pyramid: Eradicating Poverty through Profits* (New York: Wharton School Publishing).

Prasad, E., Rogoff, K., Wei, S. and Kose, M. (2003) *The effects of Financial Globalization on Developing Countries* (Washington, DC: IMF).

Pretzlik, C. and Silverman, G. (2002) 'Wall Street Under Fire', *Financial Times*, 4 October.

Prowse, M. (2003) 'Ethical decisions must be made before sciences force them on us', *Financial Times*, 5–6 July.

Pruzan, P. (2003a) 'Developing Leadership and Learning on CSR in Companies', paper presented at the second Colloquium of the European Academy of Business in Society, Copenhagen, 19–20 September.

Pruzan, P. (2003b) 'Theory and Practice of Business Ethics in Denmark', in Morsing and Thyssen (eds), *Corporate Values and Responsibilities* (Copenhagen: Samfundslitteratur).

Rabelais, F. (1993) *Pantagruel* (Paris: GF. Flammarion).

Ramade, F. (1993) *Dictionnaire encyclopédique de l'écologie et des sciences de l'environnement* (Paris: Ediscience).

Rand, A. (1996) *Atlas Shrugged*, (Mass Market Paperback).

Rawls, J. (1970) *A Theory of Justice* (Princeton, NJ: Princeton University Press).

Reno, J. (1997) *Indictment of Tobacco Industry*, (Washington: Department of Justice).

Retallack, S. (2001a) 'Mondialisation et changements climatiques', in E. Goldsmith and J. Mander (eds), *Le procès de la mondialisation* (Paris: Fayard).

Retallack, S. (2001b) 'Le Commerce mondial et l'environnement', in E. Goldsmith and J. Mander (eds), *Le procès de la mondialisation* (Paris: Fayard).

Retz, Cardinal de, (1956) *Mémoires* (Paris: Gallimard).

Rivarol, A. de (1964) *Maximes et Pensées* (Paris: Union Génerale d'Editions).
Roberts, D. and Luce, E. (2003) 'Outsourcing', *Financial Times*, 20 August.
Roche, P. R. (2000) 'L'eau au XXIe siècle', in Montbrial Th. and Jacquet, P., *Ramsès 2001* (Paris: Dunod).
Saint Augustine (1959) *La Cité de Dieu* (Tournai: Desclée de Brouwer).
Salvaggio, S. and Callis, L. (2002) *Cybersexe* (Brussels Editions Luc Pire).
Schumpeter, J. (1949) *The Theory of Economic Development* (Cambridge, Mass.: Harvard University Press).
Sénèque (1957) *Lettres à Lucilius* (Paris: des Belles Lettres).
Services du Premier Ministre (2002) *Livre blanc des acteurs français du développement durable* (Paris: Imprimerie Nationale).
Shell (1998) *Profits and Principles: Does There Have to be a Choice* (London: Shell).
Shlaes, A. (2003) 'Send farmers out to the market', *Financial Times*, 1 September.
Sinatra, A. (ed.) (1997) *Corporate Transformation* (Norwell and Dordrecht: SDA Bocconi and Kluwer).
Sinn, H. W. (2003) 'There is no European right to a place in the sun', *Financial Times*, 13 February.
Skapinker, M. (2003) 'CEO: (n) greedy liar with personality disorder', *Financial Times*, 2 July.
Skocpol, T. (2003) *Diminished Democracy* (Norman: University of Oklahoma Press).
Smets, P. F. (2002) *Ethique ou cosmétique? Le retour des valeurs dans un monde paradoxal* (Brussels: Bruylant).
Smets, P. F. (2003) *Gestion responsable et développement durable* (Brussels: Bruylant).
Smith, A. (1930) *Wealth of Nations* (London: Methuen).
Sophocle (1967) *Tragédies* (Paris: Gallimard).
Steiner, G. (1973) *Dans le château de Barbe-Bleue. Notes pour une redéfinition de la culture* (Paris: Seuil).
Stendhal (1947) *Romans et Nouvelles* (Paris: Gallimard).
Stiglitz, J. E. (2002) *Globalization and its Discontents* (London: Penguin Books).
Suez-Ondéo (2000) *Bridging the Water Divide* (Paris: Suez-Ondeo).
Tabatoni, P. (ed.) (2000–3) *La protection de la vie privée dans la société d'information*, vols 1–5 (Paris: Presses Universitaires de France).
Tabatoni, P. (ed.) (2002a) *Privacy Protection in the Information Society* (Amsterdam: ALLEA).
Tabatoni, P. (2002b) *2000–2002: La crise du modèle d'innovation aux Etats-Unis* (Paris: CERPEM, Université de Paris-Dauphine).
Taylor, F. W. (1919) *The Principles of Scientific Management* (New York, Harper).
Teilhard de Chardin, P. (1955) *Le phénomène humain* (Paris: Seuil).
Thucydides (1990) 'Discours de Périclès sur les premiers morts de la Guerre' in *Histoire de la guerre du Péloponèse* (trans. J. de Romilly) (Paris: Robert Laffont).
Tomkins, R. (2003) 'Happy birthday, globalization', *Financial Times*, 6 May.
Touraine, A. (1992) *La critique de la modernité* (Paris: Fayard).
Tristan, F. (1984) *Venise* (Paris: Editions du Champ Vallon).
Tuchman, B. (1985) *The March of Folly* (New York: Ballantine).
Tyler, Ch. (1999) Interview of Hans Kung, *Financial Times*, 25/26 August.
United Nations (1989) *Our Common Future* (Geneva: United Nations).

Urban, R. (2000) *Mondialisation et sociétés multiculturelles* (Paris: Presses Universitaires de France).

Valery, P. (1988) *Cahiers* (Paris: Gallimard).

Van den Berghe, L. (2002) Paper presented at the First Colloquium of the EABIS, Fontainebleau 5–6 July.

Van den Berghe, L. (2003) 'Redefining the Role and Content of Corporate Governance from the Perspective of Business in Society and Corporate Social Responsibility' Paper prepared for the World Economic Forum 2003 in P. Cornelius (ed.) (Brussels: Institut des Administrateurs).

Van Eersel, P. (ed.) (2003) *Donner une âme à la mondialisation* (Paris: Albin Michel).

Van Parijs, Ph. (1991) *Qu'est-ce qu'une société juste?* (Paris: Seuil).

Vienot, M. (1999) *Rapport du Comité sur le gouvernement d'entreprise* (Paris: MEDEF).

Wade, R. H. (2003) 'Held hostage by the anti-development round', *Financial Times*, 29 August.

Watkins, K. (2003) 'Reducing poverty starts with fairer farm trade', *Financial Times*, 2 June.

Weber, M. (1964) *L'éthique protestante et l'esprit de capitalisme* (Paris: Plon).

Wilsdon, J. (2004a) *See-through Science* (London: Demos).

Wilsdon, J. (2004b) Nanotech needs to listen to its public and now, *Financial Times*, 1 September.

Winter, J. (2002) *Final Report* on the *Winter's Group to M. Bolkestein* (Brussells: European Union).

World Bank (1999) *Annual Report* (Washington, DC: World Bank).

Yepès, I. (2000) 'Au Mexique, des mutations culturelles et sociales sur fond de globalisation subordonnée' in J. Delcourt and Ph. de Woot, *Les défis de la globalisation: Babel ou Pentecôte?* (Louvain-la-Neuve: Presses Universitaires de Louvain).

Zizi, M. (2003) 'Comment vivre avec le biologique pour le meilleur et pour le pire', *La Libre Belgique*, 5 May.

Index

Notes: ch = chapter, n = endnote; **bold** = extended discussion or heading emphasized in main text.